CELEBRATED CHEF MICHAEL STEVENSON

A WAY TO A WOMAN'S HEART

THE COOKBOOK

Recipes by: Michael Stevenson

Photography by: Bill Lee, Louis Pickney

Editing by: Hal Perrin

Forward by: Dr. Jessie Gee, PHD

Cover Design and Layout: BMG Marcus etc

A Way To A Woman's Heart: The Cookbook

Printed in the United States of America

16 15 14 13   1 2 3 4

Library of Congress Control Number: TXn-1-835-388

ISBN: 978-0-9844303-4-5

For discounts regarding special large orders please contact Chef Michael Stevenson at 757-338-3274 or sales@chefmike.tv
For signs and speaking engagements contact
mike@chefmike.tv
www.chefmike.tv

And so the journey begins ~ A pathway

A mysterious inward anxiousness to follow

The aroma and allure of our Hearts addictions:
Joy ,Pain, Affirmation, and Love

CONTENTS

Introduction, 13
A Way To A Woman's Heart

New Beginnings, 16
New food finds are like meeting new people.
Be adventurous but stick to your standards.

The Little Things, 37
They mean so much in food and in relationships.

Subtle Addictions, 58
When temptation runs wild, sometimes in moderation, most of the time we overindulge.
~Sinful recipes that will add pounds~

What Really Matters, 77
Every great dish starts with the best ingredients and effort.
Relationships are no different.
~Honesty, Trust, Consideration, & Passion~

Spaghetti Again, 98
Every woman can whip up this classic timeless dinner.
~The emergency meal in a glass case~

Nourishment While Being Nourished, 114
Food often tames the emotional core of all our relationships.
Food, like any great lover, is to be savored, enjoyed, and treasured.

Till Death Do Us Part, 132
Imagine life without the enchanting luscious foods of your childhood.
Imagine never having loved or been loved.
Imagine never placing your heart in harm's way.

We explore the innermost depths of your mind, body, and spirit that food can and should touch. Food, like its identical twin, love, is one of our five basic needs essential for mere survival. Thus, a life without good food and great love is not much of a life at all! Take this journey; explore and discover how to get the most value out of food and love. Our Creator, has blessed each of one of us with this mystifying gift of life! Take this trip and enjoy the priceless treasures and luxuries of both!

DEDICATION ~ TO MY FUTURE WIFE

He Who Finds a Wife Finds a Good Thing
(Proverbs 18:22)

This Desire that I have to find you and genuine Love we can call our own.

This Dream I have that I never want to wake up from your embrace.

Shadowed by this Pain I feel in my heart
Knowing that I have to embrace it to get to the other side in order to find
THE WAY TO A WOMAN'S HEART.

And to protect you from all hurt, harm, and danger, especially;
from the foolishness of a flawed man in myself.

My Prayer is that I have learned from failed relationships and can hold on
to the tiny precious Grains of Love once more—
never to let you slip through my hands.

If YOU allow me to find such a Treasure,
I will know SHE is a Special Gift from YOU.

I promise to bury HER in MY HEART so SHE will remain MY LIFE LINE.

To set HER before my eyes always so that I will never lose focus
and to always dine only in HER LOVE so that
I can grow stronger in the face of any storm.

Michael Stevenson 2013

8

ACKNOWLEDGEMENTS

My Girls, Brianna and Fridae, where in life would I be without your love? You have both shown me WHY I needed to be a better man and to mend any past hurts and misdoings. I pray that the error of my ways will never find you and your HEARTS. You are the best parts of me and my prayers are that LOVE finds you transparent and anxious. I hope you embrace LOVE, knowing that it comes with both joy and pain laughter and tears; but TRUE LOVE washes away even the deepest hurt that I cannot even protect you both from. Be true to your HEARTS for you both have been loved by a FATHER much wiser, stronger, and more consistent than Me. HE will ALWAYS be there for you and will Never Leave Nor Forsake You. I love the very HEARTS of you both and YOU make me the richest man on the face of the earth. I LOVE YOU!

My mentor Willie Moats, I knew my DREAMS were possible because I saw all that you had accomplished. You showed me that I could not only achieve but also surpass my Dreams. Spending quality time with me, mentoring me, being my friend, and teaching me, You provided me with a learning curve by being transparent in YOUR LIFE LESSONS that you shared with me. You're My Number One CHEF, friend, and mentor. I pray your happiness, health, and blessings over your family.

MOMMA, how I delight in laying on the floor awaiting each great plate of food when I come to visit. YOU NEVER DISAPPOINT! You not only have given me LIFE, but a REASON TO LIVE. Thanks to you, I am in tune with My Gifts and will ALWAYS Sing Your Praises. I AM TRULY CYNTHIA STEVENSON'S CHILD.

Dr. Jessie Gee, Shipmate, I still have your back the same as I did twenty-three years ago. Your unconditional Kindness, Love, and Excitement for this Project has RESURRECTED A DREAM lain dormant. You're a Blessing from GOD and a Treasure to Humanity. I wish YOU Love, Happiness, Health, and your Life's Desires. I will always be indebted to your kindness. Cannot wait to aid you in your Literary Ventures and Floridian Goals.

My Family and Friends: Shad, Bill, Shilon, Mike Carter, Jaybe, Almon, Charles, Chef Jay, Chef Manuel, Chef Troy, Chef Blount, Mike Cook, Vivian, Michelle (R&R Catering), Reet, Missy, Kenya, Micha, Gabby, Erna, & Corey, Deangelo and Jada Hall, Trent Williams and family, Santanna Moss and family, Fred Davis, Clinton Portis, Pharell Williams, Ludacris, Mc. Lyte, Lisa Raye, Michael Coylar, Brooke, Teddy Riley, Magic Johnson & Foundation, Guy Torre, Shang, Dale Lewis, Stacey Little John. I love you all!

MY BOYS, Caesar and Titus, YOU make me smile whenever I come home.

FORWARD

Dr. Jessie Gee, LCDR, MSC, USN (Ret)
BS Degree: Broken Heart
MA Degree: No Man Will Ever Hurt Me Again
Ph.D.: Don't Settle! Wait On GOD To Bless You.

God has blessed me with an amazing gift of communication and a surreal opportunity to travel all over the world. Thus, I have met a great variety of people from all walks of life; all with different experiences and unique perspectives. But there were two things that were always very obvious to me—out front and center no matter what country, territory, region, state, county, city, community, or home I had the pleasure of visiting.

First, and of utmost significance, is that food, indeed, is a universal language that we all clearly understand and love and are too eager to initiate conversation — even to perfect strangers! It promotes an atmosphere engulfed in fun, relaxation, and utter delight while simultaneously

engaging us in authentic communication and an assortment of relationships. Now on the contrary, with food, silence is golden and it's the highest compliment that can be paid to any passionate chef that prepared an amazing meal. Second, and equally as important, is my belief that love, food's identical twin, is craved by all mankind.

I have met men and women alike wanting to love and be loved by that perfect soul mate that "they know" is out there somewhere. Many of us, when it comes to finding that special partner—and more importantly, when trying to keep that special partner and take our relationship to the next level — often fumble, stumble, fall, or just give completely up on love and romance. We either can't figure out or don't want to follow the rules of road as we navigate through perplexing destinations along our journey to the city of LOVE, PASSION and ROMANCE. But, don't throw in the towel or hang up your apron yet!

After many years of exploration and experimentation with some of the world's most potent "food" aphrodisiacs, Celebrity Chef Mike Stevenson has masterfully refined his personal "Line of Spices" that are useful for heating up our kitchens, bedrooms, and secret meeting places. Chef Mike is a connoisseur at creating his art and masterpieces, which include lavish dishes, sensual desserts (that look too beautiful to eat), and exotic foods that will stimulate you and serve you up a steamy main course of love, intimacy, and sheer ecstasy.

Whether you're looking for love or just a great meal, this romantic cookbook will navigate you page by page to preparing a succulent appetizer, a romantic meal, and a steamy dessert of passionate lovemaking to cap off the night. Everyone — from novice to pro (or so they think, ladies) can embrace these easy-to-understand recipes and priceless nuggets of wisdom from real women who know.

Love and Food, are inseparable relationship commodities. "Culinary Art-Magician" Chef Mike coddles and blends the two sensual aphrodisiacs into one exotic cookbook masterpiece: **A Way To A Woman's Heart**. This cookbook, his second book, is another "must read" and is boiling over with luscious recipes that are sure to heat up kitchens and bedrooms around the world.

Dr. Jessie Gee

INTRODUCTION

A Way To A Woman's Heart

A Way To A Woman's Heart is a fitting title for this book. The passion and fervor of a woman's heart is something that inspires both my love for food and my desire to excel in the art of culinary expression. It is with such passion and fervor that I pursue my craft. And as a chef, I have observed an interesting phenomenon. My culinary creations, prepared with passion and care, tend to conjure up in women emotions that connect us in a mysterious but tangible way. As a man is wooed by a woman's good cooking, so a woman is wooed by my cooking. The love and romance surrounding food is paralleled by the love we exude in our personal relationships. No one dish will satisfy all customers and no one chef can tame every customer. In our preparation of food, we are charged with trying to find a pathway to people's hearts, to create emotions and memories that keep them wanting our food more and more.

I am fortunate to have grown up in a house where the flames of creative expression were fanned. I remember hearing my mother Cynthia tell me that I was a prince and I could do anything I set my mind to and I could accomplish my dreams if I applied myself. Nothing was out of reach for her "little chocolate drop," as she often called me. By introducing me to the art of food preparation and cooking at an early age, she reinforced those ideas, I think, unknowingly. Discovering that there were white cherries, and not just the red ones we see on television, allowed me to go far away in my mind to the very tree and sample them. Kiwi and papaya, pistachio ice cream and clams on the half shell… There was no "oh, Momma, I don't want that" in Cynthia's house. She made food fun, and my brother and I welcomed every new food find. Those were the days. I was blessed to have a full refrigerator most of the time and Momma kept the freezer full, too. She was the only woman that could pay the rent by selling slush drinks to the local children. When she fried chicken, it was a special day, like a holiday. I saw the love she poured into feeding the masses and I realized what would be my calling.

I wanted to be able to quiet a room with a fantastic dish, to serve mouthwatering desserts that would be talked about long after the plate was licked and then washed. I wanted to be talked about in the same admiring way as the tailor of my culinary jeans, to be so highly touted. So I dove in feet first.

Even at an early age I realized I was in awe of food and the commonality that food had with women and relationships. Although the shoe was squarely on the other foot, I saw the toughest men tamed by a plate of Momma's collard greens. They would look at her in wantonness, and I couldn't tell if they looked at her that way because she was good looking or because of the cornbread or the salmon cakes. In any event, she usually got her way. Looking back, I draw on those memories every time I am on stage in someone's kitchen. The sheer enjoyment of feeding the masses, creating magic, like Copperfield, with jumbo shrimp and allowing my audience to take part in the disappearing act was a feeling from another time.

I was a teen the first time I cooked for women and received a magical and captivating reaction. A young lady (yet older than me) worked with me. From time to time I had the privilege of seeing her at lunch. I would gaze at her, longing to be in conversation, and wouldn't you know, one day in the crowed cafeteria she sat at arm's length away from me. We started a small conversation and became friends. Soon afterward, she took ill and missed work. I found her house through her cousin who also worked with us. When she answered the door she was drenched with sweat and had a very bad cough. I asked her if it was all right if I helped her get better, and I told her that I could cook. She jokingly said, "Yeah, you're going to cook me back to health or make me worse off."

That evening I began to prepare chicken soup from scratch. I remembered how my mother Cynthia browned the bird with onions, garlic, pepper, thyme leaves, and how she added her secret brown sugar—just a pinch—to the magic cauldron. I covered the pot, allowing some of the aroma to seep into the living room where my first customer, and later my first serious emotional experience, was falling fast. After one hour I drew some of the magical broth form the sauce pan and added a little more pepper and some finely-chopped fresh spinach, and I started to feed her. She soon fell asleep. As she slept and broke some of her fever, I was in the lab fine-tuning the chicken soup—taking the meat from the bone, straining the broth, and finely chopping the carrots and the celery. When she woke, she was very hungry. After taking a shower, she was strong enough to sit up and enjoy the soup I had prepared. After eating the soup, she quickly fell asleep again. To be honest, she ate so fast that I never had the chance to ask her if it was good (but the empty bowl was a pretty good clue). Pretty tired myself, I fell asleep next to her on the couch.

I woke up to her smile. Her voice had returned, not one hundred percent, but she was in good spirits and looked at me as if to say it was my turn to talk. We spent a very feverish night finding each other's likes and dislikes. We gorged ourselves until we were spent and then she made the dessert. I had tapped into the deepest emotions of this woman through the nourishment of food. I had secured her trust by the care poured into the preparation. I was forever hooked on the idea that the way to the heart of a good woman is through the hands that prepare what touches her heart. Food is my drug and I push it. Not to seduce, though its seductive powers are seriously underrated, but I give food as an extension of myself. My expression of art… My passion, my love, and my wantonness to be loved… **The way to a woman's heart** is deep and not easily navigated. I hope that through this book we can navigate those unchartered waters and find various food treasures that make the voyage worth the stormy seas.

NEW BEGINNINGS

New food finds are like meeting new people.
Be adventurous but stick to your standards.

After spending over fifteen years cooking, traveling, and tasting some of the most amazing food in the world, I often reflect on THE FIRSTFRUIT. When a food item was unfamiliar, the introductions did not always go well and the planning was typically inadequate. The first tasting of something strange conjured up familiar memories—memories that come along with each new experience. Food has helped to shape my life in many ways and has given me unique perspectives on many facets of life. All the food items I consume (in moderation of course) continue to shape my way of life and thinking. For example, when asked, "Do you prefer this food item over that food item?" my answer is informed by my memories of past first-fruit encounters and the awkwardness that comes with them—an awkwardness that is perhaps very similar to the one that comes with entertaining a strange bedfellow for the first time.

Beginnings are hard. The unknown is what can draw people apart and make them very nearly miss the experience of the great love—or the great food find—of their lives. Then the great love consumes them, never to be released by their hold of the great love. Chocoholics can tell you when they first fell in love with the sinful aphrodisiac. They can talk of those strange encounters as it went from an unnerving awkwardness to the frequent and secret planned rendezvous to those very sensual private moments that followed.

New beginnings have always been an awkward experience; we like the familiar and tend to shy away from the unknown. Some relationships never thrive because the beginnings are so rocky. Have you ever spent time with someone who has deadlines for everything? How long is it going to take before the first kiss? How long will it take before something goes wrong? And strangely enough, something always seems to go wrong.

The beginning of a relationship should be the best and the worst of things. To put your best foot forward for one night and keep the holey socks in the closet is deceptive. You should air out your laundry early and often. If someone is attracted to you, then that person is there for more than just the cosmetics. Try to approach every new friend with honest emotions. I am not suggesting you leave your heart on a platter for someone to step on it. I am, however, suggesting that if the goal is a long-term relationship, then being transparent early on is of great value. If honesty is given and you get deception in return, that's a clear eliminator. The writing is not just on the wall, but the proof is in the pudding. I firmly believe that you have to give what you want to attract. There are a lot of winter tomatoes. You know the kind—it is bright red on the outside. At first glance, it is the perfect specimen. It adorns your plate with flawless attributes. But then the tasting begins and you quickly discover that you have been fooled. It's an imposter. Food should not be this way and neither should great relationships.

In all great cooking the best of ingredients make the best dishes. Yes, it takes effort. The flavors are not just going to combine themselves magically and produce a wonderful dish. In cooking, as in life, you get out what you put in. Take time and really understand each element. How does each flavor interact with the other? There may be something there that doesn't agree with your makeup. If so, don't eat from that plate. Relationships are very similar in that when the foods of life are placed in front of you, you don't have to eat everything on your plate. Some of the worst scenarios happen because women feel that their biological clock is ticking. There is a shortage of men. There is a shortage of great beef in today's market as well, but the great eateries don't buy cheaper beef.

It would be robbery to pass off second-hand meat as the real McCoy. Instead, we seek other vendors, do our homework, and educate our customers about the dying beef market. Yes, great beef is hard to find, but once you've had it, you appreciate the lean qualities and the great texture and depth of it. You realize that it's worth the wait. Great women, you are worth the wait. The unique way you smell and the allure that is heightened by designer fragrances. The savvy way you can turn up the heat in any situation by the provocative glances that you display in secret to your mate. But you have to keep the price steady with the market. No matter how intense a one-night stand is, there is nowhere to go afterward. You can't recover respect and sense of value after you have tainted the product. No one wants the meat that's marked with the red sticker for use the following day. It's discounted so much that you have to prepare it in twenty-four hours or throw it away. Ladies, you are more than just quick consumption, a fast-food meal to be consumed in place of a lovingly prepared culinary delight. I used to buy those discounted items and my thoughts weren't the best when shoppers who saw me in that pile of meat. It was embarrassing, and the fact is, I didn't have the money to buy prime Angus meat that was an arm-length away. The beginning of your relationship needs to be a time when the best and the worst are brought to light. Either you can deal with it or you can't. You don't want to rob yourself of a blessing, and if you're like me, you don't want to hold back anyone else.

The recipes in this chapter are the beginnings of great pairings. They inspire the desire to pair great wine and great company alike. When preparing these dishes, look at the simple things that when done right leave an honest truth about the dish. I hope that when you approach any beginning, you meet each dish and person with honest expectations. Try to discover the core of the dish and realize there's someone for everyone, just as some foods appeal to some people and others do not. And every chef can't please every customer.

Begin each day understanding what your limitations are. What do you like? What is it that really does it for you? In the relationships of life, as in cooking, invest in quality ingredients and avoid bargain shopping. Enjoy the ride and continue to explore new things. Beginnings can be great learning times for future dishes. So always keep your knife and fork at the ready.

PORTABELLA FRIES

For all the vegetarian friends in my life. They generally flock to my home when I tell them these amazing fries are on the appetizer list. The meaty taste of portabella mushrooms make my vegetarian friends forget their pledge of not consuming meat. It actually makes me think of taking the vegetarian plunge as well.

Difficulty: 1

Serves: 3

Prep:

4 portabella mushrooms
4 oz parmesan cheese
4 oz flour
2 tsp red pepper flake
1 tsp black ground pepper
2 eggs
3 oz milk
1 cup Panko breadcrumbs
4 cups olive oil

medium sauce pan

On cutting board place mushrooms, cut into quarter-inch slices, and set aside. Place 3 oz flour on serving plate. In bowl mix eggs and milk. Whisk until frothy. Add black pepper. Set aside until needed.

In separate bowl mix cheese, breadcrumbs, and remaining flour. Add red pepper flake.

Preheat olive oil in sauce pan, medium heat.

Arrange plate and bowls for breading in this order: Mushrooms, flour, egg wash, and finally, breadcrumb/cheese mixture. Toss mushroom in flour, careful not to break fries. When coated, place in egg wash, remove excess wash and place in breadcrumb mixture. Carefully ensure mushrooms are fully coated.

Repeat process until all mushrooms are coated. Place in freezer until grease is hot enough to pass fry test.
Hint. They are even better if you let them stand in freezer over night.

When olive oil is hot, administer fry test. Carefully place mushroom fries in sauce pan. Turn mushrooms to cook on both sides. Remove when golden-brown and set on draining plate.

Sprinkle with kosher salt and quickly serve with your favorite condiments.

Try a spicy ketchup or and Dijon mayo.

CAESAR DRESSING

I love the zesty, cheesy taste of this dressing. The classic pepper bite has an authentic anchovy taste without using the brined seafood buddies. Taste it and you'll be a believer.

Difficulty: 2

Makes: 1 quart

½ cup grated parmesan
⅓ cup onion white, diced
2 oz balsamic vinegar
2 eggs yolks
2 oz Worcestershire sauce
2 tsp ground black pepper
1 Tbsp roasted garlic, in juice
1 oz lemon juice
1 tsp Tabasco sauce
½ cup extra virgin olive oil
3 oz olive oil
¼ cup water
kosher salt, to taste

food processer

Prep:

In food processor, place onion, garlic, Worcestershire Sauce, lemon juice, Tabasco, Sauce, and ground black pepper.

Pulse until incorporated.

Add egg yolks and water and whip until mixture begins to turn frothy and slightly thicken.
Add cheese mix well.

Slowly drizzle olive oil and the extra virgin oil. Dressing will turn a bit pale in color.

Remove from food processer and salt to taste. Add more grated cheese, if desired.

DIJON TARRAGON HERB MAYO

One of my go-to sandwiches and dipping spreads. Very simple, but such intense flavors.

Difficulty: 1

Makes: 2 cups

½ cup Dijon mustard
¼ cup scallions, sliced
1 tsp garlic, chopped
1 cup mayo
1 Tbsp tarragon, fresh
1 tsp black pepper
2 oz olive oil
1 oz white balsamic vinegar

small bowl

Prep:

In small bowl mix:
Dijon mustard
white balsamic vinegar
garlic
tarragon
black pepper
mayo
olive oil

Mix items until incorporated.

Fold in sliced scallions and reserve until needed.

SILVER QUEEN CORN RAGOUT

Jersey silver queen corn makes all the difference in this dish. Utilize lump crab meat along with the freshest Holland peppers. You may be tempted to eat this dish right out of the pot.

Difficulty: 1

Serves: 4

2 tbsp olive oil
1 tbsp garlic, chopped
1½ cup jersey silver queen corn kernels
¼ cup red Holland pepper, diced
¼ cup celery, chopped
¼ cup sweet white onion, chopped
¼ cup green onions, sliced
kosher sea salt and pepper, to taste
6 oz lump crab meat
Old Bay Seasoning, to taste

Prep:

In large sauté pan over medium heat, pour in olive oil and roast garlic. When garlic is fragrant, add jersey silver queen corn, stirring quickly. Add diced Holland peppers, celery and onion. Continue cooking until corn is cooked through and tender. There should be a slight crunch to the celery and onion.

Add green onions to sauté pan and stir. Season with salt and pepper to taste.

Fold in crab meat. When corn ragout is hot, cover with lid and let steam for five minutes. Remove lid and sprinkle with Old Bay Seasoning. Stir and serve alongside main entrée.

- In the summer you will find an abundance of fresh Jersey corn.

- Crab meat should also be at its peak in terms of freshness.

HEIRLOOM TOMATO CAPRESE

An amazing salad if you're a tomato lover. Heirloom tomatoes are slightly more expensive than most other types of tomatoes, but well worth the experience. Pair with fresh mozzarella cheese to create a whirlwind of flavors in each bite.

Difficulty: 1

Serves: 2

3 large heirloom tomatoes
2 fresh mozzarella ovalini
¼ cup extra virgin olive oil
1 cup arugula
1 tsp kosher sea salt
cracked black pepper
½ cup aged balsamic vinegar

applewood-smoked bacon (optional)

Prep:

Wash tomatoes and wipe dry.
On cutting board, use a serrated knife to slice tomatoes into quarter-inch slices. Set aside.

Cut mozzarella cheese into quarter-inch slices.

On a large salad plate, arrange tomatoes and mozzarella cheese in a circle with alternating slices. In the center of the circle, place a nice pile of arugula leaves and drizzle 1 oz extra virgin olive oil. Sprinkle with sea salt and cracked black pepper. Finish with aged balsamic vinegar.

For an extra burst of flavor, top with crispy applewood-smoked bacon.

SHRIMP COCKTAIL

Traditional cocktail served up with a creamy cilantro avocado base. For a lighter calorie shrimp cocktail, use olive oil instead of mayo base.

Difficulty: 1

Serves: 4

12 peeled shrimp
½ cup celery, chopped
¼ cup green onions, sliced
¼ cup red peppers, diced small
¼ cup Daikon radish, diced
¼ cup mayo
¼ cup sour cream
1 ripe avocado (diced)
½ tsp ground black pepper
2 Tbsp fresh cilantro, chopped
1 tsp Old Bay Seasoning

Prep:

Cook shrimp and chill. When cooled, peel shrimp and remove vein.

On a cutting board, dice shrimp into quarter-inch pieces. Place shrimp in bowl with all chopped vegetables.

Combine mayo, sour cream avocado, fresh cilantro, and Old Bay Seasoning.
Add to bowl with shrimp and vegetables and stir to incorporate. Add ground black pepper. Refrigerate until needed.

Serve on toast or in a chilled bowl, garnished with assorted crackers.

ROASTED PEPPER HUMMUS

The amazing thing about hummus is that it can lend itself to many flavors. Experiment often or just keep it simple.

Difficulty: 1

Serves: 4-6

Prep:

1 (15-16 oz) can chick (garbanzo) peas
¼ cup sesame oil
¼ cup soy sauce
2 Tbsp lemon juice
1½ Tbsp granulated garlic
½ cup chopped roasted peppers
2 Tbsp fresh parsley
½ cup tahini paste
kosher salt, to taste

food processer

In food processer, place chick peas, sesame oil, soy sauce, lemon juice, granulated garlic and roasted peppers.
Blend until incorporated, but not smooth.
Turn off and scrape from sides. Add parsley and tahini paste.
Blend until almost smooth.
Add kosher salt until desired taste.

Add water if you want a smother paste.

Serve with your favorite pita bread or chips or use as a side tapas dish with fresh veggies.

CANDIED MIXED NUTS

A great quick snack for games, holidays, or just around the house. Very addictive and versatile.

Difficulty: 1

Makes: 3 lbs

1½ cup cashews, shelled
½ cup peanuts, shelled
½ cup walnuts, shelled
½ cup almonds, shelled
¼ cup sugar
1 cup water
1 Tbsp cinnamon
2 Tbsp brown sugar

medium sauce pan

Prep:

Preheat oven to 350 degrees.

Mix brown sugar and cinnamon in small bowl. Set aside until needed.

In large bowl, mix all varieties of shelled nuts.

Heat water in medium sauce pan on medium heat and bring to a simmer, adding white sugar. Dissolve sugar completely.
Add mixed nuts and stir until all nuts are coated with sugar water.

Place nut mixture back into medium bowl and drain excess liquid.
Top with brown sugar mixture. Toss until completely coated

Place mix nuts on baking sheet and cook in preheated oven for 10 minutes. Remove and allow to cool.

Serve warm or room temperature.

TAPENADE

I adore the texture and taste of assorted olives in my food and in one of my favorite brunch drinks, Spicy Bloody Mary. Keep the olives coming!

Difficulty: 1

Makes: 1 quart

1 cup black olives, pitted
½ cup green olives, pitted
1 tsp garlic, minced
2 shallots, minced
¼ cup extra virgin olive oil
¼ cup fresh lemon juice, plus more to taste
1 tsp red pepper flakes
salt and pepper, to taste

food processor

Prep:

Place olives in food processor. Add garlic, shallots, olive oil, lemon juice, and red pepper flakes.
Pulse until fully incorporated. Consistency should be chunky with fully blended ingredients.

Salt and pepper to taste
Add additional lemon juice, if desired.

Great side accompaniment.

CHOPPED SALAD

I delight in this salad because of its versatility. Explore and use vegetables and grains of your choice or garbanzo beans, peas, etc. Each new food find that you add to this salad will be met with thanks by your stomach.

Difficulty: 1

Serves: 2

¼ lb romaine lettuce, chopped
½ lb Iceberg Lettuce, thinly sliced
½ cup golden beets, sliced
¼ cup chick peas
¼ cup cucumbers, peeled and sliced
8 grape tomatoes
4 salad radishes, diced

handful seasoned croutons

Chardonnay Dressing: (See recipe this page.)

freshly cracked black pepper, if desired

Prep:

Place lettuces and vegetables in a large bowl.

Prepare chardonnay dressing.

Add dressing to the salad bowl and toss to combine.

Be careful not to overdress the salad. It should remain crisp.

Add croutons. Toss together.

On a chilled plate, add salad and cracked black pepper (if desired).

Chardonnay Dressing:

½ cup chardonnay wine
¼ cup shallots, chopped
1 Tbsp garlic, minced
¼ cup fresh lemon juice
⅓ cup olive oil
¼ cup cider vinegar
1 Tbsp brown sugar
2 Tbsp fresh chervil, chopped*

Add all ingredients to a mixing bowl and whisk until incorporated.

*parsley can be substituted

FIG AND FENNEL RELISH

This relish is so versatile! It can be used to stuff a chicken breast or as an accompaniment to a vegan dish. In the next recipe, we will use this relish to stuff a wonderful piece of brie. Can't wait!

Difficulty: 2

Serves: 12

2 cup fennel, chopped
¼ cup shallots, minced
¼ cup olive oil
2 cups dry or fresh figs, chopped
2 cups red wine
½ cup brown sugar
2 tsp coriander
½ cup water
1 tsp kosher sea salt

Prep:

In a sauté pan over medium-low heat, add diced fennel, shallots, and olive oil. Quickly sauté items for 2-3 minutes. Slowly add figs. Pour red wine into mixture. Add brown sugar and coriander.

Continue cooking over medium-low heat, stirring frequently. Reduce mixture until liquid is evaporated. Stir and add water until mixture is spreadable. Set aside until needed.

This is the first step to a delicious filling for the brie cheese appetizer on the next page.

FIG AND FENNEL STUFFED BAKED BRIE

The sweet, tart taste of this baked brie cheese appetizer will stand up to many varieties of wine. Start sweet and graduate to a more robust selection. You will be amazed with how the complexion changes.

Difficulty: 1

Serves: 4

8 oz brie (cut into 4 slices)
6 oz Fig Relish (See recipe on previous page.)
1 package phyllo pastry
2 eggs
3 oz water

baking sheet
sliced French bread
red wine (for consumption)

Prep:

Arrange on cutting board four evenly sliced pieces of brie. Cut brie lengthwise in half, exposing the middle of each piece. Press 1½ oz of fig relish.
Place other half of brie on top, reforming slice. Place in freezer for 15 minutes.

In small bowl mix whole eggs and add water, thus creating an egg wash. This will be used to help the phyllo pastry adhere to stuffed brie.

Preheat oven to 375 degrees.

When firm remove from freezer. Spread two pieces of phyllo sheets on top of each other. Place stuffed brie in center of sheet. Brush egg wash around edges of phyllo sheets. Alternate folding sheets over stuffed brie, completely inclosing brie.
Dip hands in egg wash and pat stuffed brie. There should be 4 rustic wrapped stuffed brie for you and your guest.

Place brie on a cookie sheet. Bake in a preheated oven for 4 minutes. Remove and serve with slices of French bread.

DRIED CRANBERRY MAYO

This wonderful slightly tart mayo is great on panini or rustic sandwiches. It can also be used as a flavorful dipping sauce for grill tempura vegetables.

Difficulty: 2

Makes: 2 cups

1 cup dried cranberries
2 oz white onions
3 oz olive oil
2 Tbsp fresh parsley
2 oz water
2 oz balsamic vinegar
½ tsp black pepper
1 cup mayo

food processer

Prep:

In food processor place dried cranberry and white onions.

Add balsamic vinegar and water.
Blend ingredients by pulsing slowly.
Drizzle oil slowly in mixture and add fresh parsley.
Remove all ingredients from food processor. Place in bowl. Add mayo to bowl. Fold in cranberry mixture.

This is the first step in an amazing journey to culinary bliss. The ultimate spread for an upcoming recipe…

Roasted Turkey Panini (See recipe on page 31.)

ROASTED TURKEY PANINI

One of my favorite sandwiches to be consumed with a great glass of red wine in the middle of the afternoon. I hope you don't have to work this day.

Difficulty: 1

Serves: 2

10 oz roasted turkey breast
4 oz arugula
3 oz caramelized onions
2 ciabatta roll (cut)
½ cup Cranberry Mayo (See recipe on page 30.)
2 oz butter (unsalted)
4 slices havarti cheese

Sandwich press or medium sauté pan

Prep:

Hint: A sandwich press will give you much better results than a sauté pan.

Option 2: Use a medium sauté pan. Cover with a thin coat of unsalted butter.

Assemble sandwiches by placing 1 oz of cranberry mayo on both sides of sliced bread. Place 2 oz of arugula on bottom pieces and top each with 5 oz roasted turkey (sliced). Place 2 slices of havarti cheese on top of turkey and 1½ oz caramelized onions. Close sandwich.
Spread each side with unsalted butter and place in preheated sandwich press.

Cook until heated through.
Cut in half and get ready for culinary bliss.

CIABATTA CROUTONS

If you have extra ciabatta bread around, try this easy crouton recipe. For all you salad lovers, it will soon be your go-to snack.

Difficulty: 1

Serves: 4

Prep:

1 loaf ciabatta bread
½ cup butter
1 tsp garlic salt
½ cup parmesan cheese
1 tsp dried parsley

Preheat oven at 375 degrees.

Cut ciabatta into half-inch slices.

Melt butter in microwave. Set aside until needed.

Place sliced ciabatta on plate. Brush with melted butter. Sprinkle with garlic salt, parmesan cheese, and parsley.

Place on baking sheet and bake until golden-brown, about 5 to 10 minutes.

Remove from oven and store until needed.

SPICE OF LIFE - I

In the beginning, women, you can't help who you fall in love with,
but you can choose who you like!

~The First Time~

The first time I met my now husband, he approached me at a restaurant where I was dining with a friend and asked if I had a boyfriend. I was, in fact, a divorcee (for several years) who was NOT interested in any man at that point, so I lied and said, "yes, I have a boyfriend". Six months later, I was out celebrating the 4th of July with family when a familiar face approached me. He reintroduced himself, reminded me of our first encounter, and asked if I still had a boyfriend. This time I told him the truth; I was a divorced, single mom. We kept in touch, talking every day and hanging out casually. One day, my best friend asked me how things were going. I told her things were fine but I wasn't sure if I wanted to date him seriously because he "wasn't my type". She said, "Your type isn't working for you. You need to give this guy a chance." Those words resonated so strongly with me because she was right.

~Deciding to Begin~

I would have been a fool to let this man walk out of my life because he "wasn't my type". I thank God for him every day. He is my best friend and my biggest supporter. We will be celebrating five years of marriage this April and there is no one else on God's green earth I would rather be with as passengers on this ride. If only we could see the heart of men! We may be able to fan the flames of love! We see with our eyes first then we feel with our hearts. When problems arise in our life we think in our minds then feel with our hearts. The heart is the key to love.

~New Beginnings~

Revelation and joy are what come to mind when I think about my first love!
All the newness of each day
Late night long phone calls that leave you breathless
Anticipation of seeing your first love walk into the room
The way your first love's hand feels in yours
Sweet perspiration and lingering scents...

A Woman's Heart: *What made your first love special?*

Ladies: *The newness of feeling something special that I never felt before.* ~Kamika Saunders

Ladies: *Revelation and joy are what come to mind when I think about my first love. All the newness of each day. Late night long phone calls that leave you breathless. Anticipation of seeing him walk into the room. The way their hand feels in yours. Sweet perspiration and lingering scents. The pain you felt when it was over, even that brings an unforgettable, irreplaceable memory. (Exhale)! No, that is not what I want to share.* ~Keisha Powell

A Woman's Heart: *What do you love most in a relationship?*

Ladies: *What I love most in a relationship is having someone that I can confide in. There is nothing greater than having someone to share your success with. I have learned over the years that not every day is going to be a great day. But, in a committed relationship, my husband is there for me NO MATTER WHAT! He appreciates my opinion and is there to share the ups and downs of life with me. These days, it's very hard to find someone that has your back. I am glad to say that I have someone that has my back. He is my number one fan and my toughest critic. Now You're Cooking!* ~Chef Dedra Blount CCI, FMP

A Woman's Heart: *What do you desire most in a partner?*

Ladies: *Honesty, open communication, and friendship. The root cause of the breakdown of a lot of relationships is dishonesty and poor communication. I want my partner to understand that honesty is always the best policy. Likewise, poor communication is the demise of a lot of relationships and marriages. For any relationship to be successful, both partners must be comfortable with articulating their feelings in a healthy open manner. Lastly, the foundation of any relationship must be friendship. When you and your partner are friends, a lot of things come so much easier, i.e. communication and honesty. When I think about spending the rest of my life with someone, I want to spend it with someone that I can laugh hysterically with, someone that I can have meaningful conversations with, and someone that I can love for an eternity.* ~Candice Jones

A Woman's Heart: *What scares you about Love or falling in love?*

Ladies: *The thought of giving someone 100% always scared me. You fall for someone and to be honest you never know what you're going to get in return. Everyone is not the same in how they handle situations and honestly I feel no one situation is completely alike. I ask myself questions when I begin to feel that four letter word creeping up. Can you deal with what your significant other is bringing or not bringing to the table is a major concern. Love changes with time. Sometimes for the good and other times it can go downhill. In some cases you have individuals who are introverts and do not communicate feelings well at all. That is the worst feeling ever to*

34

fall for someone who can't communicate what is or isn't in their heart. I've had those moments and honestly you should never have to guess what your significant other is feeling. And no one should ever make you feel that you are not worthy of knowing. But again we all handle situations differently but trust and believe it can be hard to mend a broken heart. ~Andrea JuJu Martin

A Woman's Heart: *How can your partner make you feel beautiful?*

Ladies: *The key ingredient to making a woman feel beautiful is by combining attention, affection, admiration, and adoration. It's not just about saying, "you look nice today." It's about paying attention to how she feels. It's not just about being physical. It's about intimacy—that loving hug, warm kiss and those wonderful loving looks across a crowded room. It's not about being attracted to her. It's about appreciating what she does at home, at work and within the relationship. It's not just about saying "I love you". It's about showing that love in emotion and action. If you combine those special elements, I think any women—including myself—will feel beyond beautiful.* ~Pavar Snipe

THE LITTLE THINGS

They mean so much in food and in relationships.

In every relationship the little things mean the most. Even if they are sometimes thrown aside as secondary items, the little things are generally what keep the relationship fresh and inviting. Great food is the same way. Those little morsels that have us wondering what we just consumed, or better yet, have us scouring the plate for the last crumbs of that special appetizer—these are the things that make the food appealing and keep us coming back for more. It's all about **the little things**.

Growing up in Philadelphia, my family and I would literally eat on every corner, from warm pretzels to hoagies. The smell of fresh baked goods up the block and around the corner is one of the little things that set my neighborhood apart. Little things such as this have made the most enduring impressions on me in relationships.

When someone buys you something just because they saw the smile on your face and they enjoy seeing it often… When food is less than inviting but you know that the preparer spent many hours stirring and seasoning to make it just right… When, at the end of the shift, a surprise guest brings me something other than what I just prepared for some four hundred hungry patrons…

The little things, they mean everything.

In most restaurants, the details make the difference between success or failure. The old adage, "you get what you pay for" comes to mind when I think of those establishments that fail to deliver, or those that tried to mimic the greats only to fall short. When the great ones come to the plate, they deliver a total experience that exceeds their guests' expectations. They leave their guests with a lasting impression of an assortment of little things.

Have you ever had an average meal prepared for you, yet the excellent service you received more than made up for it and you ended up enjoying the overall experience? I have had experiences like that, where the meal was slightly less than I had hoped for but still okay. And because the servers, instead of making excuses for the meal tried hard to make things right, at the end of the night I still managed to leave a good tip. We appreciate the little things. When food is prepared with passion, the little things are exaggerated and the focus is on the quality. These things form the substance of your guests' lasting memory of the meal experience.

I often ask women what makes a great relationship and one of the most common responses is "the little things." When asked to elaborate, they say, "I just want him to listen, hold my hand, surprise me every now and again." Those little things can make or break any relationship. Even though they are right in front of us all the time, we tend to ignore them or we just think they don't matter, but they really do.

Lamb chops with just the right sauce, dessert after a good meal, the right beer in the crab boil, tomatoes that you can smell before you cut them and you can taste them in your mind long after the season fades... The little things.

The little things are the great starts to every relationship and meal that is memorable. Every time I sit down to a meal I pay attention to the sauce and the garnish, and I wonder how much thought was given to these things. If you take care of the need, then the wants will be automatic. Even with my daughters, I try to take care of their needs and then their wants seem to fall into place. They are my jewels. I treasure their opinions more than the beat of my heart. The thought of being without them brings me sheer terror; it would be like trying to hold on to grains of sand as they slip through your fingers and whisper that your time is up with your dream lover.

The little things have always made me look at the world through chef-colored glasses. To be able to appreciate a hotdog and sauerkraut, a filet of ostrich, sushi with just the right amount of wasabi… The little things enable me to separate my intentions from other would-be suitors. And ladies, please keep in mind that the little things make up for the big long-term commitment, if that's what you desire. Take your time and analyze intentions. And here's some free advice, ladies, when you find the right gentleman, make an effort to let him know your intentions, because if he has stuck around through the trial-period, then his nerves could be frazzled, and a little emotional reinforcement will not hurt.

In this chapter, I will give you some little things that can be paired with main courses to enhance any meal. I encourage you to find the best ingredients available. Always keep the little things front-and-center so that you don't fade far behind. Your food—and your relationship—will be much tastier.

ASIAN BBQ SAUCE

Asian flavors are some of my favorite culinary delights. I often flock to any city that has a China Town area where I can overdose on these Eastern flavors.

Difficulty: 2

Makes: 1 Quart

1 sweet Vidalia onion (diced)
1 ½ Tbsp roasted garlic, minced
⅓ cup fresh cilantro
¾ cup hoisin sauce
2 oz soy sauce
1 cup diced tomato in juice
½ cup tomato sauce
2 oz Worcestershire sauce
3 oz honey
¼ cup scallions
1 Tbsp ginger, chopped
1 tsp red pepper flake
2 tsp chili powder
2 oz red pepper sauce
2 oz olive oil
1 cup orange juice

medium stock pot

Prep:

Preheat medium stock pot and add olive oil. When hot, add large sweet onion. Quickly sauté.
Add garlic and ginger.
Reduce heat. Stir in diced tomato, tomato sauce, hoisin sauce, Worcestershire sauce, soy sauce, and red pepper flake.
Bring to a simmer and add orange juice.
Reduce contents by half, occasionally stirring the bottom on low heat.
When sauce is reduced, add honey, chili powder, red pepper sauce, and scallions.

Bring to a rolling simmer by increasing heat. Cook until thick. Remove from heat.

Reserve Asian BBQ Sauce until needed.

For a smoother sauce, place in food processer and blend smooth.

Great on chicken (roasted or fried), pork chops, or lamb.

BRAISED ASPARAGUS WITH ROASTED GARLIC

Fresh asparagus makes an amazing side dish to any meal when braised simply with roasted garlic, olive oil, and a squeeze of fresh lemon.

Difficulty: 1

Serves: 4

2 bunches asparagus
¼ cup olive oil
4 cloves garlic, sliced
1 tsp kosher sea salt
1 fresh lemon, halved
black pepper, to taste

Prep:

Cut half an inch from the bottom of fresh asparagus. You should see the cut area weep moisture.

In a medium sauté pan, heat olive oil over medium heat.
When hot, carefully add asparagus.

Sauté for 3-5 minutes.

Add sliced garlic and sprinkle with salt. Remove from heat just before the garlic browns.

Squeeze lemon juice from both halves into the pan and let stand for 3 minutes.

Add black pepper, to taste.

STADIUM GUMBO

A weekly stadium favorite. I have upgraded this recipe to include sweet shrimp and tender crawfish tail meat. I have many clients that omit okra, but if you enjoy traditional New Orleans style gumbo, you will covet this recipe.

Difficulty: 2

Serves: 8

⅓ cup olive oil
½ cup celery, diced
½ cup onion, diced
1 lb chicken breasts, diced
1 cup andouille sausage, sliced
12 medium shrimp (cleaned and deveined)
1 cup crawfish tail meat
2 Tbsp chopped garlic
¼ cup diced green peppers
¼ diced red peppers
2 cups can chopped tomatoes in juice
3 cups chicken stock
½ cup tomato sauce
kosher sea salt
¾ cup cooked okra

Spice Mixture:
2 oz Old Bay Seasoning
2 oz ground chili
1Tbsp red pepper flake
1 tsp paprika
4 oz gumbo file
2 oz flour

Prep:

In medium stock pot, add olive oil and place the flame on medium heat. When oil is hot, add celery, onion, chicken, and andouille sausage. Cook until chicken is halfway cooked, then add chopped garlic, crawfish tail meat, peppers, spice mixture, and shrimp with tails still on. Cook gumbo file and flour into proteins.
Then add tomatoes and sauce to stock pot.
Add chicken stock, bring to simmer and allow to thicken.
Add cooked okra at the end and let stand in gumbo 10 minutes before serving.

Add kosher sea salt to taste.

Pairing:

Serve gumbo with long-grain Carolina rice or over hot water cornbread for an amazing culinary experience.

GARLIC MASHED CAULIFLOWER

When a no-carb diet is your diet of choice, try this amazing cauliflower recipe. It is sure to tame the most passionate potato eater.

Difficulty: 1

Serves: 6

2 heads cauliflower, cut into florets
2 Tbsp garlic, chopped
½ cup sweet onions, chopped
1 Tbsp fresh chervil, chopped
3 oz Smart Blend spread or extra virgin olive oil
kosher sea salt and black pepper, to taste
½ cup water
1 cup vegetable stock

Prep:

In a medium stock pot, add cauliflower garlic, sweet onion, and water and vegetable stock then cover.
Slowly bring water and stock to boil and cook until cauliflower is tender.
Drain water.

Add fresh herbs and Smart Blend spread or extra virgin olive oil to the cauliflower mixture. Whip with a fork until smooth.

Season with salt and pepper to taste.

WILD MUSHROOM RAGOUT

These earthy mushrooms combine to enhance any beef or chicken dish or as a standalone center item for a vegetarian meal.

Difficulty: 1

Serves: 4

⅓ cup olive oil
2 portabella mushrooms
1 cup shitake mushrooms
1 cup oyster mushrooms
½ cup sweet white onions, diced
3 cloves garlic, minced
¼ cup celery, diced
⅓ cup lite soy sauce
¼ cup brown sugar
2 Tbsp fresh parsley, chopped
1 tsp red pepper flake
salt and pepper, to taste

medium sauté pan

Prep:

Pour olive oil into a medium sauté pan and heat over medium heat for a few minutes.

Meanwhile, slice portabellas into quarter-inch slices. De-stem shitakes and cut in half. Remove oyster mushrooms from stem.

Place onions and celery in heated skillet. Add mushrooms to skillet and sauté all ingredients for three minutes. Add chopped garlic and cook for an additional minute. Add soy sauce, brown sugar, parsley, and red pepper flake.

Ensure you turn items in pan to allow them all to incorporate each flavor. Season to taste with salt and pepper.

When fully cooked, remove from skillet. Set aside to arrange on top of a beautiful steak or chicken dish.

SHEPHERD'S PIE

The very first time I tried this dish, I came back for seconds and thirds. I have tried to duplicate the flavors, but it's something about my mother's cooking that just cannot be duplicated. I am sure you will enjoy this recipe—full of flavors, and home cooked goodness.

Difficulty: 2

Serves: 8

2 lbs ground chuck (or lamb)
1 cup onion (diced sweet white)
⅓ cup celery (diced)
⅓ cup carrots (diced small)
4 cups mashed potato
½ cup parmesan cheese
½ cup beef stock
⅓ cup sage (fresh)
¼ cup thyme (fresh)
¼ cup brown sugar
⅓ cup red wine
1 Tbsp chopped garlic
1 cup peas (thawed)

medium sauté pan
medium baking dish

Prep:

Preheat oven to 350 degrees.

Place medium sauté pan on stove top on medium heat and add olive oil. Add onions, celery and carrots. Sauté until tender and add garlic and red wine.
Pour contents into bowl and place sauté pan back on stove top on medium heat. Place ground beef or lamb in sauté pan and cook until fully cooked.
Drain excess drippings.

Add fresh sage and thyme. Add brown sugar and beef stock. Remove from heat until needed.

In medium baking dish, sprinkle parmesan cheese on bottom layer. Cover with ground beef mixture.
Layer onions, celery, and carrots over beef mixture, including reserved juices and peas.

Warm mashed potatoes so they are easily spreadable. Carefully layer warm mashed potatoes over beef and vegetable mixture. When completely covered, sprinkle with fresh sage and more parmesan cheese. Cover with foil and place in preheated oven for 35 minutes until potatoes are bubbly and cheese is melted .

Serve hot but warn your guest that this dish retains heat for a long time.

ROASTED TOMATO BISQUE

I really enjoy a great heartwarming soup when the weather changes. This tomato soup is worth every minute spent to extract all the flavors.

Difficulty: 2

Serves: 6

2 Tbsp olive oil
12 Roma tomatoes
4 beef steak tomatoes
1 large sweet onion
2 stalks celery
5 cloves of fresh garlic
½ cup parsley, chopped
3 bay leaves
2 cups vegetable stock
2 cups water

Spice Mixture:
2 tsp red pepper flake
1 tsp paprika
1 tsp black pepper

kosher sea salt, to taste

Prep:

In medium stock pot, add olive oil and place the flame on medium heat.

Meanwhile, cut all tomatoes into quarters to allow juice and essence to release easily. Chop onion and celery into one inch pieces. Smash garlic with flat part of knife and mince. Add onions and celery to hot oil in the stock pot and cook for 3 minutes. Add the garlic and cut tomatoes and cook for an additional 3 minutes.

Pour remaining ingredients into the pot and reduce heat. Simmer for 15-20 minutes and season with sea salt to taste.

CITRUS POACHED YAMS

During the holidays, I had the pleasure of having a full house of family and guests. The crown jewel of the meal were these amazing lightly sweetened Yams bathed in fresh orange juice. With a bit of brown sugar. You and your family are in for a much healthier holiday side dish.

Difficulty: 2

Serves: 8

10 medium yams
1 cup orange juice
½ cup brown sugar
2 oz cinnamon
⅓ cup butter, unsalted
olive oil

baking dish
foil

Prep:

Preheat oven to 350 degrees.

I prefer to oil yams and roast in oven until tender. When tender remove from oven. Allow to cool for a few minutes.

Peel cooked yams and slice into half inch pieces. Arrange in baking dish. Sprinkle brown sugar over yams. Add orange juice, cinnamon, and finally butter.

Cover with foil and cook for additional 20 minutes. Remove foil and cook for additional 10 minutes.

Remove carefully from oven. Serve hot and get ready for the accolades.

I have been known to toss marshmallows on top. I invite you to try it if you can afford the extra calories.

These yams are a perfect holiday side dish. They can also take center stage at any dinner.

APPLEWOOD SMOKED BACON DRESSING

This sinfully delicious dressing is sure to be a favorite with fresh mixed greens or just simple Bibb lettuce. Keep plenty on hand if you're expecting guests to come over. If you are like me, you may have friends who can't eat bacon. I'm sorry...more for me!

Difficulty: 2

Makes: 1 quart

8 slices applewood smoked bacon, chopped
½ cup shallots, chopped
½ cup green apple, peeled and diced
½ cup olive oil
½ cup vegetable oil
⅓ cup white balsamic vinegar
2 Tbsp fresh parsley, chopped
1½ Tbsp brown sugar
kosher sea salt, to taste
¼ cup reserved bacon drippings

food processor
medium stock pot

Prep:

Place chopped bacon in a medium stock pot over low heat. This will allow for bacon to be rendered without burning.

When bacon is halfway cooked, add shallots and apples. Cook until shallots are tender and apples are soft. Remove bacon, onions, and apples from pot with a slotted spoon and place in a bowl. Measure out ¼ cup of bacon drippings and reserve in a separate bowl.

In a food processor add oil, vinegar, and fresh parsley. Place brown sugar in processer and pulse until completely incorporated.

Stop processer and add bacon, onion, and apple mixture. Incorporate until thoroughly processed. Stop processer and salt, if needed.

Drizzle reserved bacon rendering in dressing and pulse to incorporate. Remove from the processer and place into container until needed.

ROSEMARY-BRINED AIRLINE CHICKEN BREAST

Infusing fresh rosemary into this bone-in chicken breast will keep extra moisture in while cooking and the taste is purely out of this world.

Difficulty: 2

Serves: 4

4 airline chicken breast	**Prep:**
2 Tbsp fresh rosemary	
12 oz Herb Brine (See recipe on page 69.)	Preheat oven to 350 degrees.
2 tsp kosher sea salt	
black pepper	Place airline chicken breast in brine liquid for 4 to 8 hours.

Prep:

Preheat oven to 350 degrees.

Place airline chicken breast in brine liquid for 4 to 8 hours.
Note: You can brine in morning before you go to work and remove when you come home. Remove when finished brining.
Place on plate.

Season with kosher sea salt and black pepper.

Squeeze fresh lemons slices over chicken breast.

Place fresh rosemary on chicken breast.
In small baking dish, arrange grilled or roasted onions on bottom. Place chicken on top and cover with foil. Place in oven and bake for 12 minutes.

Remove foil and cook for five or more minutes until skin is golden-brown.

Remove from oven and let stand. Serve with favorite vegetable—and starch if needed.

For a sweet herb earthy taste, try a bit of honey or agave on skin of chicken when you remove foil.

4 airline chicken breast
2 Tbsp fresh rosemary
12 oz Herb Brine (See recipe on page 69.)
2 tsp kosher sea salt
black pepper
1 fresh lemon
2 large grilled sweet onions

medium baking dish
foil

CAULIFLOWER SOUP WITH CRISPY PARSNIPS

Subtle, earthy, and flavorful cauliflower is accented with a lightly salted parsnip crisp in this to-die-for soup. Make sure you invite me when you make this recipe.

Difficulty: 1

Serves: 4

Prep:

2 heads cauliflower
3 oz olive oil
1 sweet white onion, diced
1 Tbsp garlic, chopped
3 cups vegetable stock, divided
2 Tbsp fresh chervil, chopped
1 Tbsp butter
kosher sea salt, to taste
black pepper, to taste
vegetable oil
2 parsnips
kosher sea salt

food processor or blender
sauté pan

Remove stem from cauliflower and rinse in sink. Set aside until needed.

In a medium stock pot, add olive oil and sweet white onion. Sauté over medium heat for 2 minutes. Add cauliflower and chopped garlic to stock pot. Sauté until onion is translucent, then cover with 2 cups vegetable stock. Bring contents to a boil and add one more cup of vegetable stock. Add fresh chervil and cover. Reduce heat and simmer until cauliflower is very tender. Add butter and remove from stove.

Allow to cool for a few minutes, then carefully pour small amounts into a food processer or blender and puree.

This soup can be served smooth or with small bits lingering throughout the soup. Salt and pepper to taste.

In a shallow sauté pan, heat small amount of oil. Rinse parsnips. Using a vegetable peeler, shave parsnips into thin strips. When grease is hot, carefully drop parsnips in heated oil. When golden, quickly remove. Drain on paper towel and sprinkle lightly with kosher sea salt.

The crisp salty parsnips accent the mild soup perfectly.

Root Beer BBQ Sauce

This recipe was created for a Cajun menu that used reduced root beer and a hint of molasses to coat tender fried airline chicken breast topped with toasted pecans. A very yummy dining experience! I developed this recipe as the requests for the BBQ sauce grew amongst guests.

Difficulty: 2

Makes: 1½ Quarts

2 oz olive oil
½ sweet Vidalia onion (minced)
3 cloves garlic, diced
⅓ cup fresh parsley
⅓ cilantro
1 liter root beer soda or syrup
½ cup molasses
1 cup tomato sauce
⅓ cup spicy mustard
2 oz Worcestershire sauce
2 oz brown sugar
1 cup chicken stock
3 oz Liquid Smoke
1 Tbsp chili powder
2 tsp black pepper

food processor or blender

Prep:

In medium stock pot over medium-high heat, add olive oil and chopped sweet onion. Quickly sauté and add garlic.

Add cilantro, parsley, chili powder, and pepper. Reduce heat. Pour in Root Beer and Molasses. Place remaining ingredients into stock pot.

Stir sauce and simmer for about 30 minutes to reduce. When all flavors are incorporated, continue to reduce to desired thickness.

You can add a bit of cornstarch to sauce to thicken BBQ sauce. But if you have enough time, just reduce naturally.

Remove from heat and allow to cool. When cooled, place in blender or food processor and pulse smooth.

This sauce takes a bit longer on the stove to enhance its flavor.

Reserve sauce for that special Cajun meal plan.

BILLION DOLLAR CHILI

This ground bison chili recipe was developed for one of my National Football League clients. Extra lean ground bison and no beans with a spicy mixture of ground spices will certainly make this a family favorite. Be careful not to break the bank!

Difficulty: 3

Serves: 6

¼ cup olive oil
1 large sweet onion, diced
½ cup celery, diced
½ cup green peppers, diced
2 Tbsp chopped garlic
2 lbs ground bison

Spice Mixture:
¼ cup ground cumin
¼ cup ground chili powder
1 Tbsp red pepper flake
1 tsp paprika
1 (15 oz) can chopped tomatoes
3 cups tomato sauce
kosher sea salt, to taste

medium stock pot

Prep:

In medium stock pot add olive oil and place the flame on medium heat. Add the onions, celery, peppers, and garlic to oil. Quickly stir the items to incorporate flavors. Add ground bison and ground spice mixture to pot.

Cook ground bison to 155 degrees or until deep brown in color. Pour the chopped tomatoes and tomato sauce into the pot and simmer for at least 15 minutes.

Season with kosher sea salt, to taste.

Pairing:

Serve Billion Dollar Chili over short grain rice or tortilla chips, fresh cilantro, and sour cream for a southwestern fiesta.

Enjoy!

SPICY SAUSAGE DRESSING

Another addictive holiday favorite. From my family to yours!

Difficulty: 2

Serves: 8

Prep:

1 lb spicy pork sausage
½ cup chopped onions
⅓ cup chopped celery
2 tsp chopped garlic
2 cups chicken stock
4 oz butter
⅓ cup dried parsley
⅓ cup sage, fresh
1 loaf potato bread, cubed
salt and pepper, to taste

3 fresh eggs

baking dish

Preheat oven to 350 degrees.

Place sausage in a medium sauté pan over medium-low heat. Cook until sausage is halfway cooked, then add onions, celery and garlic.

Continue cooking until sausage is fully cooked. Pour chicken stock into the sauté pan and bring to a simmer, adding butter, dried parsley and sage.

Fold in cubed potato bread.
Turn gently, allowing bread to absorb liquid, onions, and celery.

Cook until all items are incorporated and bread is completely saturated and changes texture.

Season with salt and pepper to taste. Break whole eggs in dressing and mix in thoroughly.

Transfer dressing from pan into baking dish. Cover and bake for 25 minutes.

Remove foil or cover and cook for additional 5 minutes.

Tempura Citrus Lobster Bites

I generally do this recipe with shrimp. One evening my daughter Fridae surprised me with a wonderful visit. She simply adores this recipe with shrimp. Fortunately for her, I was all out of shrimp but had some lobster meat on hand. Sometimes we stumble upon the best of food finds.

Difficulty: 2

Serves: 4

1 lb fresh lobster meat
1 Tbsp fresh parsley
2 oz fresh lemon juice
¾ cup flour
1 tsp black pepper
2 tsp Old Bay Seasoning
3 oz Sprite
3 cups olive oil

medium sauce pan

Prep:

Remove excess water from lobster by squeezing and place on a plate covered with paper towel

Sprinkle lobster meat with old bay and black pepper.

In separate bowl place 4oz flour, lemon juice, fresh parsley, and a pinch of kosher sea salt. Add sprite until batter resembles a thick pan cake batter. Place remaining flour in separate bowl.

In medium sauce pan add oil and preheat until you can do a fry ready test (oil should respond when you drop flour in).

Place lobster meat in flour and coat evenly. When grease is hot, dip lobster nuggets in flour and then in tempura batter. Slowly and carefully place in heated oil. Have slotted spoon ready along with a plate with paper towel to catch excess grease.

Remove from grease when they are golden-brown. Set aside and serve alone with your favorite dipping sauce.

SPICE OF LIFE - II

~Love Addictions ~

It's not just about being physical. It's about intimacy—that loving hug, warm kiss and those wonderful loving looks across a crowded room. It's not about being attracted to her. It's about appreciating what she does at home, at work and within the relationship. It's not just about saying "I love you". It's about showing that love in emotion and action. If you combine those special elements, I think any women—including myself—will feel beyond beautiful. ~Pavar Snipe

A partner who can take charge of a situation is a major turn-on. If a man possesses these traits, I'm bound to fall head-over-heels in love with him.

~The Scent of a Woman Can Make Foolish Boys of Wise Men!~

During our truce at the end of our marriage he told me that I had an aura about me that men loved to feed off of and it drove him crazy. In my opinion, this was not my fault. I do now, at 41, understand this "aura" and I am much more careful about how I interact with men. I also realize that he was right when he told me men would just linger and hold a non-conversation just to be in my presence.

~Unconditional Addiction~

Besides God, she is the first thing he thinks about in the morning and the last thing he thinks about before bed. He proves his love more with his actions than with his words, letting nothing or no one alter his love. And finally, he shows her selfless acts of love whenever possible.

A Woman's Heart: *What personal values must a partner have to conquer your heart?*

Ladies: *Little things are what capture my heart. To me little things can change lives, you never know what someone has gone through and to be appreciative of all that comes your way is a blessing. I strive to keep a great conversation going. I love to learn and the power of growth together is a must. Being a humble person is the greatest thing ever. No one wants someone that is overly cocky all the time. Living with a purpose shows strength and the ability to get through hard times. No you don't have to have all the money in the world but have a goal in mind-- Someone who can contribute to a household, not someone who just takes all the time. Not letting your pride get in the way when it comes to anything. I am naturally a nurturer and if there is an obstacle I like to be the person who can help, but also I don't want to be the person taken for granted.* ~Andrea JuJu Martin

A Woman's Heart: *What do you desire most in a partner?*

Ladies: *In a partner I desire a "help-mate" that compliments me as much as I do him. I desire someone who has good morals and values, has a relationship with God, and LOVES love. Hopefully, they are a hopeless romantic like myself and believe in monogamy as well as a healthy relationship with consistency and good communication.* ~Stacey M.

Ladies: *Honesty, open communication, and friendship. The root cause of the breakdown of a lot of relationships is dishonesty and poor communication. I want my partner to understand that honesty is always the best policy. Likewise, poor communication is the demise of a lot of relationships and marriages. For any relationship to be successful, both partners must be comfortable with articulating their feelings in a healthy open manner. Lastly, the foundation of any relationship must be friendship. When you and your partner are friends, a lot of things come so much easier, i.e. communication and honesty. When I think about spending the rest of my life with someone, I want to spend it with someone that I can laugh hysterically with, someone that I can have meaningful conversations with, and someone that I can love for an eternity.* ~Candice Jones

A Woman's Heart: *What makes you laugh in a relationship?*

Ladies: *The little things make me laugh and smile. Crazy moments. Letting your hair down and not having to be perfect but still being able to keep a smile.*

Ladies: *Being able to laugh at our flaws and quirks. Loving the awkward crazy way we are made for each other and knowing that I can laugh and joke about my man but no other woman should dare. Pillow fights, silly pet names, worn out under garments, and mix matched socks worn around the house. I am so blessed to have a partner that can laugh out loud and we face life knowing that in spite of what horrors happen throughout our day. There is an inside joke waiting at home. You bring such joy to my heart.* ~Anonymous

A Woman's Heart: *How important is your partner's relationship with God?*

Ladies: *It is extremely important that my partner has a relationship with God. It is only through the Word of God and a true understanding of His love that we learn how to love successfully and unconditionally. God never intended for us to "fall" into anything because His Word tells us that "He will keep you from falling". His expectation is that we "grow" in love. By nature, we have learned to love based on condition, but through learning and understanding God's written Word and His unconditional love for us, I believe we will learn how to love unconditionally; without fear or regret. We will be able to forgive quickly and not hold grudges. We will not build walls of protection designed only to keep us from becoming vulnerable when in fact, that is one of the ways we confirm love. Understanding God's love and what He really sacrificed for us is the key to preventing us from hurting those who we profess our love to. We would not hurt them intentionally or unintentionally by cheating on them, abusing them (physically, mentally, verbally and psychologically), rejecting them and judging them. Without a relationship with the one who has the real power, ability and authority to change and transform us, our hope for a successful relationship/marriage is left to chance.* ~Tamu N. white

Love transforms a house into a home

SUBTLE ADDICTIONS

When temptation runs wild, sometimes in moderation, most of the time we overindulge.
~Sinful recipes that will add pounds~

To be very honest, there aren't many subtle addictions. Most are up-front and very confrontational. They tend to make the hairs on the back of your arm stand up. Sometimes they even make you travel afar in search of that seductive fix. Sometimes those middle-of-the-night cravings, those ferocious, forbidden appetites, demand to be quenched and we surrender to them. I need to place a warning on this chapter. It's not for the squeamish or weak at heart, especially not for the emotionally unstable.

My food addictions are few, but I have never been reluctant to let my likes be known. I like many kinds of food. I seek comfort in the familiar place of my food addictions and relationship addictions. They allow me to become a customer with the freedom to blame the chef for the poundage that I may walk away from the table with. They allow me to make excuses for my actions, in spite of the fact that they were premeditated. Intentions were in hiding just to be awakened in the middle of the day or night. Most people's food addictions often parallel their personal relationship addictions.

I'm not big on astrology, but I was born on the first of September and I fall under the zodiac sign of Virgo. I am passionate, I am an explorer, I am a giver. I am a hopeless romantic, which is both a curse and a blessing. I have to remind myself not to allow people to make me into something I'm not. Relationships should follow the words of your favorite love song.
Anything worth eating should be savored. Love-making should be premeditated; you should go in ready to exhaust your addictions—to satisfy and to be satisfied. Embrace your wantonness. In other words, get yours, ladies. Don't allow the man to dictate the rhythm, the flow, the music, or the bed sheets all evening. My food addictions are the same way. I don't allow many people to mess with a food I like or the way I like to eat it.

Like a great dancer during a performance, you must know when to lead and when to follow, especially during the climax of the song. And the same can be said for both a great chef and a great lover—know your part well! Do what you do to the best of your ability or just don't mess with it… For example, I like my crabs cooked in beer, fresh garlic, and with just the right amount of spice, and served with melted butter and fresh, cracked black pepper. My chocolate I like frozen, whether it's a candy bar or a piece of cake; the chill of it cures my fix. So please don't offer me warm chocolate. I come ready, premeditated. I know what I am going to order and how much. When I shop, I know I am going to spend until I feel satisfied. Exhausting my subtle addictions in this way—with passion—allows me to give to others with the same kind of passion.

Addictions can take a turn for the worse in food and in relationships. You ever had too much of a good thing? The next day or so you probably lived to regret it.

I remember my cousin coming to visit me in Virginia for the first time and eating what seemed to be a whole peach cobbler that my mother had made. We sat in awe at how he consumed every forkful. Later, he sat bent over, nursing an aching stomach and watching us enjoy our vacation. He hasn't eaten peach cobbler since.

I've had some addictions that I knew were going to get me in the worse way. Certain foods seem to keep calling me, like those fresh Thai shrimp dumplings in Philadelphia's Chinatown. Even though I knew I had to travel to a seedy part of town, I had to have that fix.

Those dumplings are intoxicating, enjoyable only by the forkful. My fix was inevitably followed by an ache similar to my cousin's. I saw it. I consumed it, too much all at once, until I finally walked away, never again wanting to see another dumpling. The very thought of it makes my teeth hurt, but it sure was good while it was going down. There are times when we need to examine our addictions, whether they are food or people, before setting ourselves up for a stomach-ache. I have been told that I try to rescue people, and so I gravitate to people whom I feel need my help on their journey. Looking back through the years, I guess there's some truth in that.

On the flip side, I am addicted to achievement and the need to have challenges and goals to obtain. I love creating things. I love great food and mind-blowing sex, not because of the addiction, but the subtlety. Every addiction can be cured if focused on. But sometimes to relish in the afterthought of a great meal or a mind-blowing intimate experience is a numbing, unmovable feeling. It's that "don't touch me right now" feeling. I think you know what I mean. It's the feeling of unadulterated satisfaction.

Hopefully, in this chapter you will discover some subtle addictions that can take you to that place of bliss. When trying these recipes, keep in mind that they are made to get you hooked. My mother always said if you play with fire you will soon get burned. Hang around this chapter long enough you will gain some addictions and possibly a few more pounds than you bargained for. I shouldn't be held liable though; you have been properly warned.

MASHED BASIL SWEET POTATOES

The versatility of sweet potatoes is shown in this recipe. They can easily be infused with different flavors. From sweet to savory. Enjoy this recipe alongside broiled fish or hearty game.

Difficulty: 1

Serves: 10

3 lbs medium sweet potatoes, peeled and quartered
1 medium sweet white onion, quartered
½ cup fresh basil, chopped
2 Tbsp garlic, chopped
2 Tbsp olive oil
½ cup vegetable stock
⅓ cup butter, unsalted
⅓ cup brown sugar
salt and pepper, to taste

baking dish

Prep:

Preheat oven to 375 degrees.

Rinse sweet potatoes and place in baking dish with onion quarters. Place in oven. Check on onions frequently and remove them when they are tender. Place sweet potatoes back in oven until they are tender and soft to touch, about an additional 45 minutes.

Carefully remove sweet potatoes. When cool enough to touch peel and place in medium sauce pan. Add chopped roasted onions, chopped basil, garlic, and olive oil to sweet potatoes.

Stir to incorporate. Slowly add stock, butter, and brown sugar and mash. Season with salt and pepper, to taste.

Place mashed sweet potatoes in a serving bowl and set aside until ready to serve.

TEMPURA MANDARIN CHILI SAUCE

Any great tempura needs a sweet tangy table mate. This is a quick, yet flavorful, sauce that enhances the crunchy texture and flavors of tempura snacks.

Difficulty: 1

Makes: 1 cup

1 small jar orange preserves
¼ cup hoisin sauce
2 Tbsp soy sauce
1 tsp red pepper flake
1 tsp ground ginger
¼ cup chopped scallions
½ tsp ground black pepper

small sauce pan

Prep:

Place all ingredients in a small sauce pan. Simmer over low heat slowly allowing ingredients to come together, for about 5-10 minutes. Stir frequently.

Allow sauce to simmer for another 5 minutes on the lowest heat.

Be careful, sauce will be very hot. Allow to cool. If consistency is too thick, add water to thin. Set aside and use as a unique dipping sauce.

Pairing:

Seafood or vegetables

LUMP CRAB STUFFED MAHIMAHI

Mahi-mahi is a mild flavorful steak cut fish—very durable and versatile. Be careful when cooking; it has the tendency to dry out quickly. In this recipe, we take the mild fish to new heights with a creamy lump crab mixture and a seasoned crust.

Difficulty: 2

Serves: 4

Prep:

4 (5 oz) mahimahi filets
½ cup parmesan cheese
½ cup butter
1½ cups Panko crumbs
2 tsp black pepper
2 tsp Old Bay Seasoning
⅓ cup mayo
1 cup lump crab meat
1 Tbsp Dijon mustard
¼ cup fresh parsley
kosher salt

baking sheet

Crab Mixture:
Place cleaned crab meat in bowl. Add Dijon mustard, mayo, 1 tsp Old Bay Seasoning and 1 Tbsp fresh parsley. Mix until creamy and all ingredients are incorporated. Set aside until needed.

Breading:
In separate bowl, mix Panko crumbs, cheese, black pepper, Old Bay Seasoning, and a pinch of kosher salt. Set aside until needed.
Melt butter in microwave and set aside in bowl.

Mahimahi:
Preheat oven to 350 degrees.
Place filets on cutting board. Cut each filet in half lengthwise. On bottom half of filet, place 2 oz of the crab mixture in center.

Make a slit in center of top piece of mahi-mahi. Be careful not to break the top piece in half. Drape center slit over mound of crab mixture on bottom piece. Repeat this step until all mahi-mahi are stuffed and ready for breading.

Place stuffed mahi-mahi in melted butter. Shake off excess and place in Panko crumb cheese mixture.

Coat completely and place on baking sheet. When all are coated, bake for 25 minutes or until internal crab is hot.

PARMESAN CRUSTED TILAPIA

The versatile fish is flavor enhanced by quickly frying it with a crust of bread crumbs, herbs, and salted cheese. Need we say anymore? You can substitute any firm white fish.

Difficulty: 2

Serves: 6

12 filets tilapia
1½ cups seasoned breadcrumbs
½ cup cornmeal
½ cup grated parmesan cheese
2 tsp black pepper
3 whole eggs
½ cup milk
2 oz hot sauce
vegetable oil (for frying)

medium sauce pan

Prep:

Egg Wash:
Mix whole eggs and milk together with hot sauce. Set aside until needed.

Breading:
Incorporate all dry breading items: seasoned breadcrumbs, parmesan cheese, and cornmeal. Set aside in bowl until needed.

Tilapia:
Season with black pepper and kosher salt. Place in egg wash and allow to soak for a few minutes. In medium sauce pan, heat vegetable oil.

When grease has passed the fry ready test, remove tilapia filets from egg wash and place in breading. Coat both sides. Shake off excess and place in heated oil.

Turn down heat and cook until golden-brown. Remove fish when fully cooked and place onto draining plate.

I generally serve fish hot, right out of the grease. There is nothing better with or without side items!

SLOCUM'S FRIED CHICKEN

This recipe was actually taught to me by my cook mentor at a country club early in my career. And yes, his name was Slocum. This was some of the best fried chicken I have ever had the pleasure of consuming. I am sure you will agree.

Difficulty: 3

Serves: 6

Prep:

1 whole fryer chicken, cut into individual pieces
1 Tbsp Old Bay Seasoning
⅓ cup hot sauce
1 tsp black pepper
2 tsp seasoning salt
ice
1 cup water
vegetable oil, for frying
2 cups flour
2 Tbsp garlic pepper
1 Tbsp salt

Tip: The key to great fried chicken is dredging the frigid chicken in the seasoned flour and cooking evenly in oil until juicy and fully cooked, but still golden-brown on the outside.

Place all the cut-up chicken in a large bowl. Place Old Bay Seasoning, black pepper, and hot sauce on chicken. Sprinkle seasoning salt into chicken mixture.

Cover chicken with ice. Add cup of water and set in refrigerator for an hour, allowing the chicken to get frigid. Meanwhile, combine flour, garlic pepper, and salt in a mixing bowl or a large zip-top plastic bag.

In a large sauce pan over high heat, add vegetable oil and heat.

Remove chicken from refrigerator. Remove each piece and add to seasoned flour. Dredge in flour with hands, shake off excess flour and place in heated vegetable oil. Place no more than five pieces in heated oil.

Reduce temperature to medium heat and cook for 12 to 15 minutes. Check by pricking chicken. This will also allow oil to penetrate bone of chicken. Remove when done and place on draining plate. Repeat until all chicken is cooked.

POTATO CHIP CRUSTED CRAB CAKES

This style of crab cakes was introduced to me by my chef mentor and best friend Willie Moats. I still travel miles from home in order to dine at his table. He utilized a different binding method that is a kitchen secret. Sorry!

Difficulty: 2

Serves: 4

1 lb lump crab meat
¼ cup Holland pepper
2 Tbsp chives
½ cup mayo
2 Tbsp Dijon mustard
½ tsp black pepper
2 tsp Old Bay Seasoning
2 bags kettle potato chips

medium sauté pan

Prep:

In a medium bowl, mix mayo and Dijon mustard.
Clean lump crab meat, making sure there are no shells or debris. Place chopped chives, Old Bay Seasoning, black pepper, and Holland peppers (diced) in cleaned crab meat.
Mix all ingredients. Add mayo/mustard mixture and incorporate to a creamy firm constancy.

In a separate bowl, crush kettle chips. Drop 2 oz of crab mixture in broken kettle chips. Firmly mold cakes with kettle chips, ensuring that each crab cake is fully coated. Repeat until all crab cakes are made. Place crab cakes in the refrigerator for 10 minutes.

Preheat oven to 350 degrees.

Heat olive oil in medium sauté pan. When oil is hot, carefully place crab cakes in pan, searing until golden-brown. Turn and cook on other side. Repeat until all crab cakes are seared.

Place crab cakes in oven while preparing the rest of your meal.

Heat crab cakes through until hot internally and serve.

BRAISED BEEF SHORT RIBS

When I am not under time restrictions, I usually surprise my NFL clients with short ribs. I often take the liberty of preparing a few for my home as well. The meat is tender and flavorful. It pairs well with a robust red wine and hearty starches.

Difficulty: 3

Serves: 4

3 lbs short ribs
2 onions, chopped
½ cup celery
1½ cups red wine
1½ cups vegetable stock
2 oz Worcestershire sauce
1 oz soy sauce

Dry Mix:
¼ cup coriander
1 tsp white ground pepper
1 Tbsp kosher salt
2 tsp red pepper flake
½ cup brown sugar
1 tsp chili powder
2 Tbsp dried parsley

Prep:

Preheat oven to 325 degrees. Rinse short ribs and lay on cutting board. With a sharp knife, make crisscross patterns in short ribs. This will allow the season to penetrate more easily.

In a small bowl, combine dry mix ingredients. Liberally rub dry mix into pores of short ribs shaking off excess. Place on plate. Set aside until needed.

In medium sauté pan, add olive oil. When hot, carefully place short ribs in searing seasoning into meat. Sear for 5 minutes and turn over. Repeat process and remove to lined baking dish.

Place celery and onion in sauté pan, and render.
Deglaze pan with red wine and pour on top of short ribs.
Place parsley, carrots, and garlic.
Add ½ cup vegetable stock and bake in oven for 3 hours. Check for tenderness of short ribs. They should be tender to touch and not shredding apart.
Remove from oven, drain stock, and let cool down.

Assembly:

In small sauce pan, strain beef wine stock to 1 cup vegetable stock and bring to boil. Slowly thicken with cornstarch for a gluten-free sauce that will bring the short ribs to life. Add 2 cups Mushroom Ragout (see recipe on page 43).

Cut short ribs into 4-oz pieces. Heat in stove. When ready, arrange on plate and top with wild mushroom ragout and a few ounces of sauce.

Serve with whipped mashed sweet potatoes for a savory comfort food experience.

LOBSTER SLAW WITH TERIYAKI SHRIMP

I don't think much needs to be said in support of an all-star cast like lobster and shrimp. Simply amazing flavors! I just hope that I am invited when you cook this dish.

Difficulty: 2

Serves: 6

1¼ lb lobster meat
2 cup napa cabbage
½ cup red Holland peppers
⅓ cup sweet onion (sliced thin)
¼ cup fresh cilantro
¼ cup white wine
Old Bay Seasoning, to taste
black pepper, to taste

24 medium shrimp
3 oz soy sauce
1 Tbsp chopped garlic
1 Tbsp fresh parsley
½ tsp red pepper flake
⅓ cup pineapple juice
olive oil

medium sauté pan
roasting dish (small)

Prep:

Fill medium bowl with warm water.
Cut napa cabbage into half-inch pieces. Chop in half and place in water, allowing any debris to fall to bottom.

Peel and devein shrimp. Place in zip-lock bag. Pour pineapple juice and add red pepper flake and chopped parsley into bag. Add soy sauce and brown sugar. Chill until needed.

Preheat oven to 350 degrees.

In medium sauté pan, add olive oil. When hot, add onion, peppers, and garlic. Toss in chopped cilantro.

Add cleaned napa cabbage and sauté until tender. Add lobster meat. Season with Old Bay Seasoning and black pepper. Deglaze with white wine. Remove pan from heat.

Place shrimp in baking dish and bake for 10 minutes.

Remove from oven and cover with lobster slaw.

Return to oven until shrimp are cooked and heated through. Remove baking pan from oven, place lobster slaw on bottom of plate, and arrange teriyaki shrimp around.

CAJUN FRIED TURKEY

This very addictive preparation of classic turkey is another favorite must-have dish. Around the holidays, showcase the golden bird alongside a traditional oven roasted turkey and see who crosses the finish line. Everyone is a winner in this race!

Difficulty: 3

Serves: 12-15

Prep:

12 lb fresh turkey, or frozen turkey completely thawed
⅓ cup fresh parsley
2 Tbsp Cajun spice
6 oz butter (melted)
1 Tbsp garlic, granulated
¼ cup Tabasco sauce
2 tsp black pepper
1 Tbsp kosher salt

peanut oil
electric turkey fryer
marinade injector
baking dish
foil

Preheat oven to 350 degrees

Fill electric fryer to limit line with peanut oil. Preheat oil. When light goes off, its ready.

Note: Ensure fryer is level.

Melt butter, garlic, and spices in pan. Strain butter and reserve in cup.
Place injector in cup and draw butter into injector. Inject butter into breast in three different areas.

Repeat butter injecting into the leg and thigh areas as well.

Take garlic and residue from butter mixture and rub on skin of turkey.
Add fresh parsley, pepper, and salt.
Set in refrigerator until needed.

When grease is hot, place turkey completely submerged in grease. Cook for 40 minutes. Remove carefully and set on drain plate.

Transfer turkey to carving or serving plate and be sure to keep a leg for yourself!

FRESH HERB BRINE

This quick brine is perfect to infuse multitudes of flavors in poultry. In less than six hours you can infuse depth and core flavors that will change the way you think of various poultry.

Difficulty: 1

Serves 6

20 oz warm water
4 bay leaves
½ cup sugar
½ cup red wine vinegar
½ cup chopped cilantro
¼ cup chopped rosemary
½ cup chopped parsley
1½ Tbsp kosher sea salt
2 Tbsp chopped garlic
1 Tbsp ginger
1 tsp paprika
1 tsp black pepper

Prep:

In a container used for brining poultry, place all ingredients. Slowly pour in warm water.
Stir until sugar and salt is dissolved. Let stand until poultry is prepped and ready to be used.

Rinse the fowl to be cooked (internally as well). Be sure to remove any debris inside.

For larger poultry, cut poultry in half. Spread open breast. Lay fowl in brine. Let stand for at least 6 hours. (If you brine in morning, by the time you return from a day's work, your dinner is ready to be cooked.)

When brining is completed, remove from brine and discard used brine. Season poultry as desired and cook until desired doneness.

SPICE OF LIFE - III

~Subtle Addictions~

Being able to adapt to change in gender roles helps to ease stress,
leaving more time for the good stuff!

In the beginning of my marriage, I didn't expect my husband to assist or share in household
chores and cooking unless he wanted to. This had a lot to do with my upbringing, which shaped
many of my views as it pertains to the role of man and woman. As our family grew, I began to feel
overwhelmed and burdened. I began to resent the times that he stopped after work to have a drink
or went upstairs after saying his hello until dinner was ready.
I did not know how to express my feelings.

~Seven Commandments of a Good Husband~

1. My husband never lets anyone take advantage of me.

2. My husband constantly tells me how proud he is of me.

3. If I am burning the candle at both ends, my husband makes me slow down and rest.

4. My husband holds my hand whenever, especially during prayer.

5. My husband always runs my bath water and washes my back.

6. I never have to put gas in the car, because my husband always takes care of it.

7. My husband doesn't wait until special holidays to buy for me.

Strength of character is high on the list of women.

It usually comes down to the strength of his character and his integrity,
how he handles life and the choices he makes.

We all encounter challenges in life and our relationships.

We all experience successes and failures,
but if we feel our partner is not to be counted on during the hard times,
we lose faith in them.

A Woman's Heart: *How does a woman know if her partner loves her?*

Ladies: *The first time I met my now husband, he approached me at a restaurant where I was dining with a friend and asked if I had a boyfriend. I was, in fact, a divorcee (for several years) who was NOT interested in any man at that point so I lied and said, "yes, I have a boyfriend". Six months later, I was out celebrating the 4th of July with family when a familiar face approached me. He reintroduced himself, reminded me of our first encounter, and asked if I still had a boyfriend. This time I told him the truth; I was a divorced, single mom. We kept in touch, talking every day and hanging out casually. One day, my best friend asked me how things were going. I told her things were fine but I wasn't sure if I wanted to date him seriously because he "wasn't my type". She said, "Your type isn't working. You need to give this guy a chance." Those words resonated so strongly with me because she was right.* ~Shilon Anderson

Ladies: *The moment I knew this man was in love with me was when I took a trip with my daughter to Canada. I hesitated to go because my mother was ill and I didn't want to be out of the country if something happened. However, the trip was paid for and it was past the point of getting a refund. He assured me that he would check in on my mom when her husband and my brothers were unable to. One day during my trip, I got a call from him saying that he had stopped past my mother's house and that she was doing fine. I thanked him and hung up.*

Later, my mother called me in tears. Through her tears, she told me how he was her guardian angel. She said she was so sick and weak that after getting out of the tub, she had to lie on the floor in her robe because she was too weak to stand. She said she heard someone calling her name from the front door but was too weak to answer loud enough for him to hear. My now husband, concerned because he knew my mother was home alone, came into the house, found her on the bathroom floor, carried her to bed, laid her down, fed her soup, and gave her the medicine she needed.

In that moment, I knew that this man loved me. He showed me through his actions that day. Although he had only been in my mother's presence a few times, he did not hesitate to help her out of his love for me. To top it off, he was so humble about what he had done. He showed me what type of man he was on that day and has proven it every day since. I would have been a fool to let this man walk out of my life because he "wasn't my type". I thank God for him every day. He is my best friend and my biggest supporter. We will be celebrating five years of marriage this April and there is no one else on God's green earth I would rather be with as passengers on this ride called life. ~Shilon Carter Anderson

Ladies: *I believe a woman knows that her man loves her by being made to feel secure on all levels of the relationship. Besides God, she is the first thing he thinks of in the morning and the last thing he thinks about before bed. He proves his love more with his actions than with his*

words, letting nothing or no one alter his love. And finally, he shows her selfless acts of love whenever possible. ~Ky Ziegler

Ladies: *A woman knows. When you are in a relationship with a person and you grow together, you know and feel a connection with your partner, and as time moves on, you grow to love each other. By the way a man treats a woman you can clearly tell if he loves her or not. I have been married 11 years and I can truly say that I know that my husband loves me. I see it in his eyes, I feel it when he is around me, and I see how he treats me. Love is a beautiful thing and I personally think everyone should experience it. My husband came into a ready-made family and he stepped up and was a father figure to my children without hesitation, and that made me love him even more. He always showered me and my children with love, and they loved him from day one. I never doubted his love for me, and only see him loving me more and more.* ~Carmen Smith

SMOKE HOUSE GRILLED VEGETABLES

These vegetables will add flair, healthy taste, and nutritional value to any meal or outing. Try different combinations of vegetables for your own unique grilled blend.

Difficulty: 2

Serves: 4

6 baby zucchini
8 asparagus, cut in thirds
4 shallots, cut in thirds
2 Holland peppers, yellow and red, cut in one-by-one-inch pieces
4 portabella mushroom, cut in one-inch strips
2 green onions, cut one-inch strips
1 tsp chili powder
2 tsp roasted garlic
½ cup olive oil
1 tsp smoked paprika
2 oz lemon juice
kosher sea salt
black pepper
¼ cup fresh sage

outdoor grill
medium sauté pan
small baking dish

Prep:

Marinade:
Place olive oil in shallow bowl and add all dry spices, fresh herbs, and lemon juice.
Toss in with cut vegetables.
Allow to sit for 20 minutes.

Grilled Vegetables:
Heat outdoor grill and season grates with olive oil.
Remove vegetables from marinade and place on heated grill. The vegetables may flash due to the oil-based marinade. Move them around on the grill to reduce flash.
Sprinkle with kosher salt and cook until heated through.
The vegetables should have a great smoky taste and still have some crunch left.
Serve hot and enjoy

If cooking indoors:
Preheat oven to broil at high temperature.
Heat medium sauté pan.
Remove vegetables from oil-based marinade and place in heated sauté pan on medium heat.
Season with kosher sea salt.
Quickly sear.
Remove from sauté pan and place into baking dish. Place in preheated oven and broil on high for 5 minutes, allowing vegetables to char.
Remove and serve hot.

CHILLED CRAB PASTA SALAD

Light lunch salad to be shared just between friends and great conversation with a glass of champagne in the middle of the day. Celebrate life!

Difficulty: 1

Serves: 3

1 cup lump crab meat
¾ cup king crab meat (remove from shell)
2 oz celery
3 oz green onions
⅓ cup radish
2 cups small shells
1 Tbsp parsley (fresh)
2 tsp Old Bay Seasoning
½ tsp black pepper
1 tsp kosher sea salt
⅓ cup lite mayo
⅓ cup sour cream
3 eggs (boiled cut in slices)
2 tsp olive oil
1 tsp lemon pepper
flat bread crackers

medium stock pot
large bowl

Prep:

In medium stock pot, fill halfway with water, add oil and a pinch of salt. Place over high heat. When water boils, add small shells. Quickly stir to ensure they don't stick.

When fully cooked, rinse under cold water and coat with 1 oz olive oil. Set aside until needed.

In large bowl, mix pasta and mayo/sour cream mixture. Add scallions, celery, and sliced radishes. Sprinkle with Old Bay Seasoning, black pepper, and salt to taste.

Mix crab meat and sprinkle with lemon pepper and a teaspoon of olive oil.

When ready to serve, arrange on plate with sliced boiled eggs. Sprinkle pepper and top with lump crab and king crab mixture.

Garnish with salted flat bread crackers.

APPRECIATION

Thanks to the all the woman throughout the world who sacrifice their lives and themselves each day to make their partners, children, and the universe a whole lot better to live in! Thanks to the following ladies from across the nation of various backgrounds who participated in **A Way To A Woman's Heart**.

A Special Thanks To:

Shilon Anderson .... *New Jersey*
Dedra Blount .... *Virginia*
Patricia Cato .... *South Carolina*
Flavia Cologan .... *Pennsylvania and California*
Altha Mae Davis .... *South Carolina*
Rhonda DeMoulin .... *New Jersey*
Vonetta Dumas .... *Washington DC*
Melissa Fayson .... *New York*
Nina Garrett .... *New Jersey*
Angela Green .... *Alabama*
Aletha Harper .... *Arkansas*
Cynthia Epps Harrison .... *South Carolina*
Tonja V. Hicks .... *Kansas*
Portia .... *Virginia*
Candice Jones .... *Washington DC*
Irene Johnson .... *Mississippi*
Andrea "JuJu" Martin .... *Maryland*
Stacey McNeil .... *Texas*
Toni Mendrick .... *New Jersey*
Kesisha Powell .... *California*
Kamika Saunders .... *Pennsylvania*
Pavar Snipe .... *Virginia*
Carmen Smith .... *Georgia*
Tamu white .... *Delaware*
Deidre Vinson .... *California*
Ky Zeigler .... *California*
Numerous other women across the country who desire to remain anonymous...

Ladies and gentlemen, as promised, the summary of the demographic data collected is as follows:
1. Hundreds of women across the nation from diverse backgrounds helped breathe life into our quest to bridge the gap between relationships, love and romance.
2. Age Group of Participants: 26 years to 83 years young
3. Geographical Region: From metropolitan New York to sunny California and many states in-between. A sample of states is listed above.
4. Relationship Status: Single, Engaged, Never Married, Happily Married, Not-So Happily

Married, Not Sure, Hanging On By their Toe Nails, Divorced, & Widowed.

5. I'm thrilled to report that all our ladies are gainfully full-time employed. Way to go, ladies, in this current economic crisis! Who said there were no jobs out there? According to these ladies, not only are there jobs in the market, but great jobs. Numerous ladies are self-employed as well as working another 40-hour work week.

6. Educational Level: As a professional researcher, this is one of the most diverse, motivated, and educated population of ladies that I've had the pleasure of working with. We sampled education levels ranging from only completion of Middle School to Post-Graduate Degrees, including Vocational and Technical Training. In addition, many of the ladies are currently working full-time, top-level positions, while simultaneously pursuing additional educational goals to improve themselves spiritually, emotionally, financially, economically, and personally.

7. Race: Thanks for the great enthusiasm for our unique cookbook. We were able to reach across most racial and ethnic lines. We left no lady behind. No matter who you are, where you reside, or what you do, I'm pretty sure that there is someone in this book who represents your thoughts, beliefs, perspectives, and life experiences, whatever they may be.

8. Occupational Positions: You will discover a broad range of career fields, not limited to, but to include: our precious moms and homemakers (we can't live without you), students, business owners, TV hosts, writers, clergy, chefs, teachers, hair stylists, retirees, state and federal government employees, healthcare professionals, and business executives, just to name a few.

9. Economic Levels: Annual household incomes ranged from less than $10,000 to over $150,000. It is sheer delight and a wonderful blessing to see that the majority of these women broke through that darn "glass ceiling" that has been hanging over our heads in the workplace ever since the beginning of time. Yes, so much for that "dead dinosaur", for not only have these ladies lifted it and cracked it, but their data clearly indicate that they have crushed it, once and for all! We are not turning back, and as you very well know, fellas, there's no stopping a strong and determined woman on a mission.

10. Homeownership vs. Renting: Who said that there was a housing bubble destroying our good ole America dream? Not according to these ladies. An unbelievable 95% of our ladies own their homes, and this also includes our single ladies. Hats off too you all! So, guys, are you taking notes? Do you need to borrow our pens? What these data indicate is that not only are these ladies across America intelligent, financially secure, and independent, but also extremely responsible and know a thing or two about handling their business and the importance of having and maintaining good credit—a priceless commodity and precious jewel! You certainly can't buy a house or much else without it these days. Great job, ladies. Lead the way for our youth, young adults, and seasoned folks. Also lead the way in taking this recession by the gonads. Share the love and wisdom you have obtained with anyone hungry enough to listen, and make this nation a better place for us all.

Finally, our sincere thanks once again to all of you. We look forward to seeing you at a book signing in or near your city. Thank you!

Chef Mike Stevenson & Dr. Jessie Gee

WHAT REALLY MATTERS

Every great dish starts with the best ingredients and effort.
Relationships are no different.
~Honesty, Trust, Consideration, & Passion~

In the art of food preparation, expression is the driving force behind each dish. Whether it's a fast-food empire or a BYOB (bring your own beverage) that awes the community standing in line to dine, they both come alive due to their expression. We embody these traits also when we dine in each. What really matters is that people are allowed to express themselves in truth and honesty. Even if it hurts, the revealed truth is the foundation that allows others to make informed decisions. If deception is in the forefront, then decisions are being made without the correct information.

Many a restaurant has failed because the identity is tainted. They start out with a clear direction and then a short time later, when the tables are not full, someone has a grand idea. "Let's try to be like the place up the street that has them standing in line." They change the menu, start promoting drink promos that are similar to their nearest competitor, and welcome in the crowd. Then the patrons, upon coming in, notice that the seafood dip they loved—and just brought in three guests to sample—has been removed from the menu. They later realize that the drink menu is just like Charlie's up the street. But when thinking of Charlie's, they suddenly want what Charlie has on his menu instead of what they originally came in to try. So off to Charlie's they go. I'm not saying you should not look at your competition to assess what the market is doing, but if you look at the world on a whole, you will see that there is something for everyone and that your niche is yours, exclusively for you to perfect and take people along for the ride. I very rarely watch cooking shows, not because I think they are not creative, but because I choose to read and allow my mind and palate to drive the creative process. It's what really matters, individual expression of truth.

When people first meet me they say two things, they speak of my love for people and then the drive and passion I have for food. I express my inner self through food and through interaction with my clients. My daughters understand that their dad is driven by his passion and that he sometimes forgets to call at specific times but will call by the end of the night. (That's a problem I am working on.) I am honest about food, but I refrain from critiquing the masses. I understand that the opinion of the masses is needed to create a service for someone else who likes what the masses have to offer. I love it when someone cooks for me or shows me new food or ways to eat. I just appreciate the effort that it takes.

What really matters in relationships is the freedom of expression and the ability to embrace differences. Often men think in terms of the perfect woman, sometimes dubbed the "dime piece". Often being so shallow, we offer the dime status because of the exterior view. But people, like onions, have many layers that often make us cry the deeper we are allowed to go and the longer we are exposed to the fumes. At times, the beliefs and the mannerisms of the partner make the deal sour and we want to leave our plate in search of something more appetizing. Often we dine and are afraid to order a new dish. We say things like, "I am not going to waste my money on something that I don't even like." You just may have passed up the best dish ever, but as the saying goes, what you don't know won't hurt you. We've all ordered something because it looked good in the picture on the menu only to be disappointed when it is served; it looks miserably less than the picture. Great dishes speak to what is advertised about them. To order crab cakes and get more cake than crab is a letdown. Personally, I stay away from crab cakes unless I am dining at one of my chef friend's establishments, because I like crab and don't want the disappointment. It's funny how many times people get connected with the intentions of trying not to get involved. It's like eating chocolate cake every day and saying you are not going to gain weight. It's a short-lived fantasy. Love comes when you least expect it. A great dish comes the same way. You have to sift through the menu sometimes in order to uncover the gem that you have overlooked so many times before.

On the flip side, you have to live up to the advertising. I read a quote by Margaret Thatcher that spoke of power. "With love being the most powerful force, I believe in the world." Excuse me if I take the liberty to amend her quote.

Being in love is like being a lady. If you have to say you are a lady, you just may not be.

In other words, people should see that glow that comes from romance and that nervous glow of expectation of seeing your partner. Be on the inside what you display on the exterior. Don't be a winter tomato, you may just attract the same crop. When food is done right, it silences the masses. At a dining experience with friends, I sat humming and silent, and when I looked up, my friends were wondering what was wrong with me. I jokingly said that all was well, that I am concentrating on the moment, and that the food makes me sing on the inside. I often tell cooks that the best complement that a room full of guests could give me is silence at the end of the meal. That tells me they are so consumed by the food that they are in bliss.

These recipes are straightforward fare; they need no help winning your heart and palate. Keep in mind that the purest dishes are the hardest to prepare because every detail is vitally important to the success of the dish. What really matters is that you express your likes and dislikes, what you will and won't tolerate, and how many dishes you're going to wash before you scream. Just have fun, because I'm sure that there are many pitfalls that life will give you.

A Woman's Heart: *Is there a difference between "love" and "in love"?*

Ladies: *I believe the difference between "love" and being "in love" in a relationship is quite simple. You can love someone but not be "in love" with them. You can love your family, friends or pets. However, if you are "in love" with someone, you are in a romantic relationship. You think about this person romantically all the time. I am fortunate to still be "in love" with my husband after knowing him for a long time and being married for eight years. He is my best friend, a passionate person, and a wonderful husband. He is my rock, and I can't imagine living my life without him.* ~Kamika Saunders

A Woman's Heart: *What makes a woman fall out of love with her partner?*

Ladies: *I think a woman falls out of love with her partner because she stops respecting him. It may be because she discovers he cannot be trusted. It usually comes down to the strength of his character and his integrity, how he handles life and the choices he makes. We all encounter challenges in life and our relationships. We all experience successes and failures, but if we feel our partner is not to be counted on during the hard times, we lose faith in them.* ~Toni Mendick

Ladies: *For me, when a man is jealous of my accomplishments, that causes the love to dwindle. I understand fully that people in general have insecurities about things, and sometimes MANY things, so it is expected that issues will need to be worked through in any relationship. The problem is when such insecurity causes jealousy from the one who I should be able to show all your strength to. This is part of selflessness in a relationship. I had a 4 ½ year-old child when I married my ex-husband. He thought that his love for me would cover EVERYTHING, but it did not. As we traveled down the 9-year road of marriage, it became more evident that the saying "love conquers all" was not true. An example would be how he would push my son away and jokingly say "get off my wife" when we hugged or kissed or showed affection; that really hurt me. Then when I expressed how this made me feel, he did not care enough to try to see it my way. He just continued the behavior that caused a riff. Also, when he exited the military and I was able to get jobs that made more money than him, he was jealous. It did not make me see him in any different way, but it seems like he saw himself in a particular way.*

I also remember when we would often have dinner parties, we would debate about "women in the military" or other topics that turned into heated discussion. Oftentimes, we ended up on opposite sides of the fence, but the debate would be fun and it would really rev me up for some up-close and personal time with him, BUT it did not take me long to realize he would be steaming mad! When our guests would leave, he would say things like "you just had to be against me, didn't you?". Until I caught on to NOT do this, my answer would be "I would never have guessed you would find that to be offensive".

Another example would be when in a large fellowship setting, a conversation would break out, and lots of times I would be the center of attraction. A conversation would start and branch off into sections, and sometimes my conversation would draw more attention, and later I would be reprimanded for talking so much. Another example would be my interaction with males; he would often say to me "why are you always in some guys' face?", and this really perplexed me because we went to a church of about 500 members and I would talk to the husband AND wife at the same time. Not to mention, WE had very close relationships to a lot of people.

During our truce at the end of our marriage, he told me that I had an aura about me that men loved to feed off of and it drove him crazy. In my opinion, this was not my fault. I do now, at 41, understand this "aura" and I am much more careful about how I interact with men. I also realize that he was right when he told me men would just linger and hold a non-conversation just to be in my presence. I remember when I graduated my Associate's degree and my ex said to me "that is nothing, it is just a community college". Can you imagine my allowing this to really affect me?! I became slightly depressed and did not appreciate my accomplishment. Then I woke up and said to myself, "At least I can check the box 'yes' when the application asks do you have a degree." I had to really re-evaluate myself because he was tearing at the very fibers that made me who I was.

He would often tell me he understood why it was that black men went to white women. It was because they "supported" their man. He expected me to just allow him to pursue dreams (that were not based upon research of their possibilities of becoming reality, but just whimsical ideas or passions). While I am a dreamer as well, I am a realist who understands that a dream needs the support of a document commonly referred to as a college degree. After 9 long years of marriage and many revelations. ~Tonja V. Hicks

GRANNY SMITH APPLE BREAD PUDDING

I really enjoy the simple flavors of good home cooking! Is there any better way to finish off a meal than with a bowl of warm bread pudding, topped with a scoop of your favorite ice cream?

Difficulty: 2

Serves: 8

6 granny smith apples
1 loaf potato bread
2 tsp cinnamon
1 tsp nutmeg
6 large eggs
3 cups milk
½ cup brown sugar
½ cup granulated sugar
½ cup golden raisins

Prep:

Preheat oven to 350 degrees

Rinse granny smith apples and dice. Set aside until needed.

Cut potato bread loaf into half-inch pieces and place in a greased rectangular baking dish. Sprinkle cinnamon and nutmeg over bread.

Crack eggs in medium bowl and add milk. Pour in sugars and stir until incorporated.

Pour wet mixture over bread in baking dish. Toss in diced apples, and golden raisins. Fold until mixture is completely saturated.

Cover with aluminum foil and bake for 30 minutes in preheated oven.

Remove foil and bake an additional 5-10 minutes, until fully cooked and golden-brown.

Cool or serve hot with your favorite ice cream. Enjoy.

BLACKENED NEW ZEALAND LAMB CHOPS

If you love lamb but are hesitant to prepare it on your own for fear of a gamey taste, this recipe is just for you.

Difficulty: 2

Serves: 3

2 lamb racks
coarse black pepper, to taste
olive oil, for drizzling

Blackening Seasoning:
¼ cup chili powder
¼ cup garlic salt
1 Tbsp white sugar
1 Tbsp dried parsley
2 tsp paprika
¼ cup olive oil

Prep:

Preheat oven to 350 degrees.

On cutting board, place rinsed lamb racks. On back of lamb chop racks, score (or make crisscross incisions) on fat part of lamb chops. Season chops with coarse black pepper and olive oil. Sprinkle lamb chops with blackening seasoning. Let stand or rest in refrigerated area for 20 minutes. Remove and prepare to sear.

Heat ¼ cup olive oil in a medium sauté pan over medium heat. Carefully sear fat side of lamb chops. Be sure not to over-char the lamb chops or it will take on a bitter taste. Rotate lamb in sauté pan searing entire lamb chop. Remove and place in baking dish.
Bake for 25 minutes in oven.

Remove from oven and place hot baking dish on covered surface. Carefully remove lamb chops and place on cutting board. Slice each chop from rack.

Serve with your favorite pasta or vegetables.

GRASS-FED VEAL PARM WITH PUREE EGGPLANT

Italian flavors abound in this classic preparation. Roasted eggplant puree is a perfect back drop. Great company and an a amazing wine seals the deal.

Difficulty: 2

Serves: 4

Prep:

Veal Parm:
4 veal chops (boneless)
2 eggs
3 cups breadcrumbs, seasoned
4 oz parmesan cheese
3 Tbsp fresh basil, chopped
2 tsp dried thyme
1 tsp black pepper
4 oz olive oil
Marinara (See recipe on page 100.)
6 fresh mozzarella slices
flour

On cutting board, place rinsed and dried veal chops. Lay plastic wrap over cutlets. Carefully pound chops until ¼-inch thick. Pound all and remove from cutting board, season with black pepper and ground thyme.

In separate bowl, mix breadcrumbs and parmesan cheese. Place in fresh chopped basil. Set aside until needed. Crack both eggs in shallow bowl and whisk with 3 ounces of water. Place olive oil in large sauté pan. Heat until fry test is complete. Place seasoned chops in flour and then in egg wash. Drain excess and place in bread crumb mixture. Firmly pat breading onto both sides.

Puree Eggplant:
2 eggplant, diced
⅓ cup red wine
2 tsp chopped garlic
1Tbsp oregano
¼ cup onion sweet (diced)
½ tsp red pepper flake
⅓ cup vegetable stock
kosher salt, to taste

medium sauce pan
plate with paper towel
baking sheet

In heated sauté pan, cook veal chops on both sides until golden-brown. Remove from pan and drain on paper towel. Place on baking sheet. Top with fresh marinara. Place a slice fresh mozzarella cheese and more fresh basil. Place in oven until cheese is melted. Remove from oven and serve with your favorite pasta or vegetables.

Puree Eggplant:
Cut eggplant in large cubes and place in medium sauce pan. Turn on medium heat. Add olive oil and onion, and sauté. Add fresh oregano and remaining seasoning. Pour in red wine and simmer until tender. Add vegetable stock and cook until soft. Take fork and break apart eggplant into chunky texture. Add salt and pepper, to taste.

A great backdrop for the veal.

CUBAN BLACK BEAN SOUP

A hearty fall or winter soup. Keep this recipe as is for a vegan specialty, or add spicy sausage or ham for a robust meal. Enjoy it with fresh baked crusty bread!

Difficulty: 1

Serves: 4

1 bag dried black beans
½ cup white onion
½ cup celery
¼ cup cilantro
2 Tbsp chopped garlic
5 cups vegetable stock
6 Yukon gold potatoes, quartered
⅓ cup Holland peppers
¼ cup cumin
1 tsp chili powder
1 tsp black pepper
1 tsp white sugar
3 oz olive oil

large stock pot
blender or food processer

Prep:

Place dried black beans in warm water for 15 minutes allowing them to bloom a bit before you start the cooking process.
In medium stock pot, add olive oil.
Throw in onion, celery, and chopped garlic. Quickly sauté until onion is tender.
Remove black beans from liquid and place in sauté pan.
Add cumin, chili powder, half of vegetable stock, and cilantro. Cover and simmer for 20 minutes. Add remaining vegetable stock and quartered potatoes. Add sugar and cook until black beans are tender and potatoes are as well. When all ingredients are tender, carefully pour a cup at a time into blender or food processor. Puree all ingredients to desired consistency.

Return to stock pot and bring soup to a simmer. Add kosher salt, to taste. Place diced Holland peppers for a fresh bite and texture.

For an additional flavor boost, sauté spicy sausage in sauté pan and ladle over black bean soup.

Serve hot with fresh-baked crusty bread.

Golden Beet, Cucumber, and Tomato Salad

My mother introduced me to this salad at a very young age. It reinforced my love for fresh vegetables and simple ingredients. I generally eat at least two salads a day and this is almost always one of them.

Difficulty: 1

Serves: 4

4 golden beets, washed, cooked and cooled
1 English cucumber
2 ripe beef tomatoes
⅓ cup red onion, very thinly sliced
1 Tbsp fresh parsley

Dressing:
½ cup cider vinegar
¼ cup olive oil
¼ virgin olive oil
¼ cup water
1 Tbsp brown sugar
1 tsp red pepper flake
1 tsp fresh parsley
1 tsp garlic salt

Prep:

Peel cooled beets. Cut into quarters.

Peel cucumber, if desired. Cut in half lengthwise, then slice.

Cut the tomatoes into 8 wedges each.

Prepare dressing as stated, below.

Place the cucumber and red onion into a bowl. Add the fresh parsley and prepared dressing. Then add the golden beets and tomatoes to the bowl. Toss all ingredients to combine flavors. Chill until serving.

Dressing Prep:
Place all ingredients in a bowl and whisk well, until thoroughly incorporated.

CRISPY SALMON CAKES

My mother would make these for me most mornings, alongside hot scrambled eggs and fried potatoes. After this delicious breakfast, I would wish I could go back to sleep. Instead, I would head out the door for school with a happy and full belly!

Difficulty: 2

Serves: 4

12 oz premium salmon (Canned salmon actually works better. If you have leftover cooked salmon, surely use it. It will only enhance the flavors.)
1 oz green scallions, sliced
2 oz sweet white onions (small diced)
2 oz celery (small dice)
1 Tbsp Dijon mustard
⅓ cup mayo
1 large egg
2 cups Panko crumbs

medium bowl
sauté pan

Prep:

In medium bowl, break up cooked salmon, completely separating the protein. Add diced onions, celery, and green onions. Toss in seasonings and fold together. Pour in Dijon and mayo mixture. Add egg. Completely incorporate all items. Contents should be glossy and should stick together.

Place Panko crumbs in separate bowl.

Using a small spoon, scoop out 3 ounces salmon cakes into Panko mixture. Completely coat cakes with Panko and pat firmly into small cakes. Set aside until ready to cook.

Cooking Method:

In shallow sauté pan, add olive oil. When oil is heated, carefully place salmon cakes in pan.

Cook until golden-brown and turn over to other side for about 3 minutes.
Salmon cakes should be heated through, but if not, place on baking sheet and place in preheated oven at 350 degrees for 5 minutes.

Serve alongside other brunch items or as standalone memorable afternoon snack.

86

OLD BAY SHRIMP DEVILED EGGS

For the holidays, I try to take traditional favorites like deviled eggs, and place a modern twist on them. I stumbled upon this recipe at Thanksgiving when we had a surplus of stuffed shrimp. So, we simply sautéed the remaining shrimp, and added to our deviled eggs. We were all pleasantly surprised with the result.

Difficulty: 1

Serves: 12

1 doz large eggs
2 Tbsp vinegar
2 Tbsp Dijon mustard
⅓ cup mayo
2 tsp chives, diced (plus more for garnish)
2 Tbsp olive oil
6 large shrimp
1 tsp Old Bay Seasoning
kosher sea salt, to taste
black pepper, for garnish

medium sauce pan

Prep:

Fill a medium sauce pan with water and bring to a boil. Carefully place in whole eggs. Cook for 3 minutes. Remove pan from heat and run under cool water. Peel eggs and set aside.

Combine vinegar, Dijon mustard, mayo, and chives in a small bowl. Set aside until needed.

Pour olive oil into a medium sauté pan over medium heat.

Meanwhile, peel and devein shrimp. When olive oil is hot, add shrimp. Sprinkle shrimp with Old Bay Seasoning . Quickly sauté until fully cooked. Remove shrimp and place on a cutting board.

Roughly chop and set aside until assembling deviled eggs.

Assemble Method:

Cut peeled eggs in half. Arrange firm white halves on a decorative plate.

Place cooked egg yolks in Dijon mustard-mayo mixture. Mash egg yolks with a fork and stir to combine mixture.

Carefully fill each egg half with yolk filling. Repeat until all eggs are filled.

Sprinkle filled eggs with black pepper and additional chives, if desired. Garnish with chopped shrimp.

Set before your guests and watch these delicacies disappear!

BOURBON BBQ GAME HENS

One of my favorite dishes incorporates tender fresh game hens, brined for 8 hours in smoky bourbon and spicy BBQ marinade, and then oven-roasted to perfection.

Difficulty: 3

Serves: 4

3 cups water, divided
⅓ cup cider vinegar
1 cup Asian BBQ Sauce (See recipe on page 39.)
2 fresh game hens
½ cup bourbon
1 large sweet onion, sliced
1 Tbsp fresh rosemary
1 Tbsp chopped garlic
3 oz cider vinegar
3 cups water
1 tsp black pepper
2 tsp kosher sea salt

Prep:

Preheat oven to 375 degrees.

Dress game hens first by opening and removing from package. Rinse and remove fresh pouch from inside cavity of game hens. Place on cutting board. Cut game hens through breast opening cavity, laying flat. Salt and pepper inside cavity. Place in roasting dish for brining.

Place 2 cups of water in deep baking dish. Pour in vinegar and Asian BBQ Sauce. Rub on skin of game hens. Prick the skin with a fork or knife so the sauce can penetrate through to the flesh. Pour in bourbon. Let stand for 8 hours covered in refrigerator. (Tip: Prepare in the morning before work. They should be ready to cook when you return home.)

Remove from brine, rinse baking dish, line with foil, and place game hens in dish, cavity side down. Top with onion, fresh rosemary, and chopped garlic. Sprinkle with black pepper. Add remaining 1 cup water to bottom of baking dish. Cover with foil, place in oven, and cook covered for 20 minutes. Remove foil and cook for an additional 8 minutes until skin is golden-brown.

Assemble Method:
Remove game hens from baking dish and place on cutting board.
Cut through back bone and arrange half on each plate.

Serve with traditional side dishes.

CURRY TIGER SHRIMP SATAYS

A delightful seafood appetizer. Create different options using your favorite vegetable combinations.

Difficulty: 1

Serves: 4

24 tiger shrimp
1 medium red onion
2 green peppers
1 Tbsp ginger
2 Tbsp cilantro
⅓ cup curry paste
⅓ cup milk
1 tsp kosher sea salt
¼ cup lime juice
1 oz mint chopped

wooden skewers
olive oil

medium sauté pans

Prep:

Rinse and peel tiger shrimp. With a small sharp knife, devein shrimp. Rinse shrimp to remove any debris. Place in bowl to marinate.

Cut onions into pieces, starting in the center and cutting each side into four pieces, totaling eight. Cut green peppers into half-inch strips and place with onions.

In medium sauté pan, add olive oil. When heated, quickly sauté onions and peppers tossing in ginger, lime juice, and mint. Remove and allow to cool. Vegetables still should have a firmness to them.

Take wooden skewers and place deveined shrimp at one end. Alternate onions, green peppers, and shrimp on the skewers. Each satay should have three shrimp on each.

Place in shallow baking dish and add chopped cilantro. Mix milk with curry paste and kosher sea salt. Pour over shrimp satays.
Ensure satays are fully coated .

Let stand for thirty minutes in refrigerator.
Preheat oven to 350 degrees.

Remove satays from refrigerator. Place on baking sheet. Cook uncovered until shrimp are fully cooked, yet still moist.

Serve over rice or as a standalone appetizer.

BIBB BLEU CHEESE AND BACON SALAD

I really can't put my addiction to blue cheese into words. Sweet, smoky flavor of the applewood-smoked bacon is layered between a subtle backdrop of fresh Bibb lettuce. Sliced tomatoes create a fresh contrast that brings all the flavors into balance.

Difficulty: 1

Serves: 4

2 heads fresh Bibb (Boston) lettuce
6 slices applewood-smoked bacon
1 cup Point Reyes Original Blue (or other bleu cheese brand, as desired)
2 beefsteak tomatoes
½ cup sour cream
⅓ cup mayo
¼ cup white balsamic vinegar
1 Tbsp cane sugar
2 tsp coarse black pepper
1 tsp dry mustard
¼ cup fresh parsley, chopped
olive oil
⅓ cup red onion, sliced thin

baking pan (for bacon)
large bowl
4 small bowls
cutting board

Prep:

Preheat oven to 350 degrees.

Arrange bacon on baking dish. Place in preheated oven. Cook bacon until crisp. Remove from oven and cut into half-inch pieces. Save oil from bacon for dressing.

Dressing:
Place sour cream and mayo in bowl. Throw in fresh parsley, cracked black pepper, vinegar, 2 oz bacon rendering, olive oil, dry mustard, and sugar. Mix all ingredients. Add bleu cheese and mix.
Let stand at room temperature.

In shallow bowl, rinse lettuce to ensure the debris is removed. Shake off excess water.

Rinse tomatoes and place them both on cutting board. Remove core and slice tomatoes in quarter-inch slices.

Cut lettuce heads in quarters. Arrange in bowl, placing lettuce down first.
Next, place tomatoes slices, then sprinkle with dressing. Add bacon pieces and bleu cheese crumbles. Top with more fresh parsley. Lastly, place thin slices of red onion before serving.

MY MOMMA'S COLLARD GREENS

If you happen to run into her, please don't tell her that I used some of her trade secrets. When she cooks collard greens, my culinary world stops. Simply mouthwatering!

Difficulty: 1

Serves: 10

5 lbs collard greens
3 bunches mustard greens
2 lbs kale
12 oz smoked turkey meat
1 small sweet onion
⅓ cup vinegar
¼ cup Tabasco sauce
2 Tbsp chopped garlic
2 Tbsp kosher sea salt
2 tsp coarse black pepper
water
3 cups vegetable stock
2 tsp garlic powder
4 tsp seasoning salt
2 tsp lemon pepper

large stock pot
large slotted fork or tongs

Prep:

Fill sink halfway with warm water and add kosher sea salt. Place collard greens on cutting board and cut into one-inch strips and then cut into two-inch pieces. Place in warm water, allowing to float.

Remove stems from kale and mustard greens. Cut in 4 places, add to sink half filled with warm water. Let stand for twenty minutes. This will draw out debris and allow the grit to fall to the bottom of the sink.

In large stock pot, add olive oil and chopped smoked turkey meat. Remove all greens from water and place in draining pan. Carefully add greens half at a time to stock pot. Cook each amount down and sprinkle with garlic powder, seasoning salt, and lemon pepper.

Repeat process until all greens are cooked down. Cover with vegetable stock and water. Pour in vinegar and cook until liquid is removed by half. Cover again with water and bring to a simmer. Pour in Tabasco sauce and cook until greens are tender.

Remove from stove top and serve. Enjoy!

Note: Greens can be frozen once cooked.

WILD RICE STUFFED SALMON

I have to admit that I need to create interesting pairings for me to sit and eat salmon. This dish is not only super good for you, but the health benefits alone should make this a staple meal. Please enjoy as I try to consume more salmon dishes each year.

Difficulty: 2

Serves: 4

Prep:

4 (5-oz) salmon filets, fresh (Atlantic, King or Sockeye)
1 tsp kosher sea salt
¼ cup olive oil
1 tsp garlic, chopped
¼ cup sun-dried tomatoes, chopped
⅓ cup sweet white onion, chopped
½ cup wild rice
kosher sea salt, to taste
2 cups water
½ cup mandarin oranges, in juice
4 cups arugula
fresh Italian parsley

Place salmon filets on cutting board. With sharp knife, carefully cut salmon in half lengthwise. There should now be 8 pieces. Sprinkle with Italian parsley and 1 teaspoon kosher sea salt. Set aside until needed.

Heat olive oil in a medium sauce pan over medium heat. Add garlic, sun dried tomatoes, and sweet white onion. Quickly sauté, add wild rice, and season to taste with salt. Stir to incorporate all ingredients. Cover rice mixture with water and bring to a boil.
Cover sauce pan and place on low heat. Cook until wild rice is bloomed and still has a bite to it and water is absorbed, about 30 minutes.
Remove from heat.

Preheat oven to 350 degrees.

Remove salmon from refrigerated area. Place wild rice mixture in center of bottom piece. In reaming pieces of salmon, insert knife and make an incision through middle of fish, keeping fish intact. You are creating an opening that can lay on top of bottom pieces of salmon. Place fish on baking dish. Add mandarin oranges in juice and remaining rice. Surround fish, cover, and cook until fish is done in preheated oven.

Place over a bed of sauté arugula and enjoy this healthy meal.

MAINE LOBSTER, JONAH CRAB, AND SHRIMP COCKTAIL DISPLAY

Have a craving for seafood? This easy fun recipe is sure to amaze and delight your friends and family. Be sure to save some for yourself.

Difficulty: 2

Serves: 4

Crab Boil:
⅓ cup Old Bay Seasoning
10 oz lager beer
1 Tbsp red pepper flake
½ bunch parsley
1 lemon
4 cups water

4 whole garlic cloves
2 lbs red bliss potatoes
8 petite corn on the cob
2 whole Maine lobsters
12 Jonah crab claws
20 shrimp
1 Tbsp fresh parsley, chopped
½ cup butter (unsalted)

large stock pot
4 whole garlic cloves

large serving bowl (long and shallow)

Prep:

Start crab boil in large stock pot and bring to a boil. When boiling add whole garlic. Rinse and quarter red bliss potatoes. Place in stock pot and cover for 12 minutes. Remove cover after 12 minutes. Add fresh corn, whole Maine lobster, and Jonah crab claws. Cover for 5 minutes. Add shrimp and remove from heat. Remove potatoes and corn. Remove lobster and crab claws. Allow shrimp to stand in hot water until fully cooked.

On cutting board, deconstruct lobster, removing tails. Cut in half with a sharp knife. Place in serving bowl. Add potatoes and corn. Place crab claws on cutting board and carefully crack the back of claws with back of knife. Add to serving bowl. When fully cooked, remove shrimp and add to serving dish. Bring broth left in stock pot to a boil and add a few cups to serving dish. Add parsley and unsalted butter and call in the troops.

Tip: Make available some melted butter, cocktail sauces, and plenty of ice-cold beverages.

SPICE OF LIFE - IV

What Really Matters

Lack of trust is a deal-breaker.

I feel secure in a relationship when I feel that I can totally trust my partner.

Taking a woman's heart and love for granted is a dangerous mistake men make too often!

A woman's heart is very fragile, and her love should never be taken for granted.

A spiritual relationship is on the hearts of most women's list...

I think it is very important for my partner to have a relationship with God.

Quality time equals a quality relationship.

Spending time together means more to me than any store-bought gift.

A Woman's Heart: *What do partners need to understand about a woman's heart?*

Ladies: *Partners need to understand that a woman's heart is as strong as nails but more fragile than a snow flake. It can carry the heaviest of burdens. When she allows the walls of protection to come down, she expects her love to protect it at all costs. A woman's heart is tolerable. It can withstand the heaviest storm. Its only request is that the storm isn't created by the one assigned to protect it!* ~M. Fayson

A Woman's Heart: *What makes a woman fall in love with her mate?*

Ladies: *A good man who cares 200% PLUS about his lady and doesn't care who knows it. He's a jewel to be treasured who goes out of his way each and every day to make sure all her needs are met before he ever thinks of considering his own needs. He tells hers at least once a day that he loves her and how much she means to him. He makes her feel special when she feels she has lost her way and not the woman she used to be or has the potential to be. He knows how to make her smile when she is sad. He makes her laugh when it's all she can do to hold back the tears of pain that she endures. He protects her when she feels threatened. He makes her secure when she feels insecure. He holds her hand and opens her doors. He acknowledges everything she says or does whether it's big, small, right, wrong or indifferent—knowing she means well. He encourages her when she feels like not going on another moment. He gives her beauty for her ashes of life. He is her shelter during the storms that each turbulent day brings. He provides her with peace in her life of chaos. He is her sunshine during the rain. He is her "bright summer day" when Old Man Winter comes knocking at her door. He is her candlelight in the still darkness. He gives her nourishment and water when she is physically, mentally, and emotionally starved and thirty for better days and a better Life. He shows her there is hope for tomorrow when she fails to see pass today. He reassures her that Old Man Trouble, Heartache, and Pain surely don't last always. No, he is not GOD and can't replace God in her/our lives. But surely, possibly this "man" knows God intimately and has been mentored by our Heavenly Father, Lord Jesus Christ on how to treat a lady—every lady—mother, sister, & friend!*

Ladies: *I love a man who loves and cherishes his mother, for that is how he will treat me. A man with a servant's heart who won't hesitate to help others tugs at my heartstrings. A mate with a sense of humor is a must, I love to laugh. And a partner who can take charge of a situation is a major turn-on. If a man possesses these traits, I'm bound to fall head-over-heels in love with him.* ~Anonymous, Metro Washington DC area

Ladies: *When a man loves a woman—gives love, makes love, and knows how to receive love without fear of being or appearing too sensitive, and all that other nonsense many of them grew up being taught by men who were clueless on how to love and treat a lady. Also, like many women I know, we want to fall in love with a "good, honest, faithful, Christian man" who loves* the Lord and treats everyone good—a man who does "unto others as you would have them to do unto you". ~Aletha Harper

A Woman's Heart: *Is love enough to sustain a relationship. Why?*

Ladies: *No, I don't believe that love is enough to sustain a relationship. I believe with my whole heart that love is from God and it is His will that we love each other. However, He never said it would be easy to love. There has to be patience when bearing with one another in love. Meaning that there will be times in our relationship we need to consult God first in all matters of the heart. There must be forgiveness in the relationship, because we are not perfect people, we will mess up. And then there is sacrifice, one of the hardest things to do when you don't want to give in. In past relationships, it was all about me, and I felt that I was due to have that one thing or the man that I wanted to be with. But this was not the will of God. In His Word, He says "a man that findeth a wife, findeth a good thing", not a woman who findeth a husband. We see with our eyes first then we feel with our hearts. When problems arise in our life, we think in our minds then feel with our hearts. The heart is the key to love. We must chase after God with our whole heart so that He can give us the desires of our heart. This, with love, will help us to sustain our relationships. ~Patricia Cato*

A Woman's Heart: *What do you desire least in a partner?*

Ladies: *I HATE A LYING MAN!* ~Aletha Harper

96

SPAGHETTI AGAIN

Every woman can whip up this classic timeless dinner.
~The emergency meal in a glass case~

The old stand-by meal, as some people may refer to it, has been this time-honored pasta dish. Spaghetti… It has been passed down through the ages and given to the masses of women in a glass case. Their teachers tell them that if you have to cook something, then this will do the trick. Then they affix a label that says, "break in case of emergency." Has such a time-honored dish been reduced to the emergency stand-by meal, thrown together when there's no time to make a "proper" meal? Only in America… I think it has been known to save a marriage or two.

The entire Italian community would be in an outrage because we defile their classic dish. The love and vigor they put into this dish and their approach to it should be applauded. It's not just noodles in some sauce. It's pasta and tomato gravy. To call it a stand-by meal would be blasphemy in the typical Italian family. This dish would take center stage at weddings, funerals, and every festive occasion. Caterers would gladly and proudly deliver it again and again not because they were bored or ran out of ideas, but because they approached it with love, and once again, with a premeditated recklessness. To find love in a dish over and over is the true pinnacle of passion for food. To make love to someone new is so much like the stolen cookie situation; it's great because it's not yours. But, the true artisan finds delight in baking the same style bread over and over, perfecting each batch. Waking up early, measuring the ingredients to exact quantities, and hoping there's little humidity in the air… And that's even before the baking begins. As a former baker, I can tell you that the care that goes into baking brings such joy when your bread is proofing. You know you've done it right when you've taken the care to protect the product's integrity. When it comes out from the oven, it's birthed with care and forethought enough to be worthy for all to see.

I grew up alongside Italian friends who would make gravy. They selected the tomatoes first, not just any fruit, but the very best. The ancients would say that you should smell the tomatoes upon walking into the room. Gravy tomatoes could have some blemishes, but they couldn't lack character depth. Why does this sound so much like a life partner? Like good lovers, the tomatoes had to be made of good stuff; the flavor extraction process would be long and intense, so they needed to be able to stand the heat. Onions would be sweet and young, able to give off just the right amount of contrast, and then harmonize with their crimson buddies. No detail was overlooked in the selection of produce. And, of course, every great gravy maker would give you a history lesson about the pot they used and why.

Once all the ingredients were selected, only cold water would be used. Every chef knows that the best and purest sauces are derived from pure, unhampered bases. Hot water, traveling through boilers and heat refiners, could add unwanted sediment to foods in preparation, tainting the sauce. We certainly would not want that. But in the United States, we take this shortcut, time and time again, by preparing produce with hot tap water. We do the same in relationships. What's hot for the moment? The varsity football player or the guy who's great in math and science…? Who's going to listen to you when you need him to? On the surface, the brawny guy seems like the obvious choice and may appear to meet the need of the moment. But even in his cold state, the intellectual guy might be the best liquid for the recipe in the long run.

Noodles aren't just pasta unless that's how you see them. You have the power to bring the dish to life if you approach the food preparation with the same vigor as you pursue your relationships. Of course, you don't always get out what you put in. If I told you otherwise, I would be deceiving you. But, if you take the time to select great ingredients, carefully blend them, continuously stirring and placing a pinch of this and a pinch of that, then you can create some magical moments—moments that may be able to be bottled and handed out as wonderful gifts. The time you invest in that relationship, whether it was for a lifetime or a summer romance, could be the basis for a romance novel. The care you put into the process and the intense flavor extractions are going to come out in the end, and you will be the better chef and person for it. You may not always get the kudos, but you will know that you have fed many people with the loving gifts of your hands. Hopefully, in the not-too-distant future, you will get to enjoy a home-cooked meal that will have been prepared with such care, or at least be taken out to a great eatery that compares. I will be the first to say you don't have to be a great chef to take care of me and my needs; you just have to have great effort and desire, backed with good old want-to-do-it.

You will be surprised how much cooking you can do if you just want to do it. The toughest question ever presented to me was, "How do you fall in love with cooking?" The people on my staff are not trained chefs, but they will have great resolve and effort to go the extra mile or they won't last long; at least not in my kitchens. They will all learn what it takes to make a little thing beautiful and look for the best ingredients in the recipes and in the ventures and the people they associate with. Life recipes are frequently dissected in my kitchens. Spaghetti is served up quite a bit. We never get tired of it, due to the fact we approach it with a fresh glance. We look to make it better than the last time by upgrading the components, like making a better selection of meats. Maybe just placing it in a different bowl could be the thing that enhances the enjoyment of the meal, like making love at a different time of day. Be deliberate and calculating. Know your pasta and know your tomato gravy. I'm convinced that if everyone who has an emergency spaghetti dish in a glass would take the time to make tomato gravy from scratch, just once, if they would take the time to become intimate with every aspect of the ingredients in the process, then they would fall in love with their new creation and never again return to their old quick spaghetti. I strongly recommend you try this same intimate process used in making great tomato gravy when making love to your life partner. Set aside some time to explore your partner's desire. Know your partner intimately in every way. Set aside time to deliberately send them sexually to the moon without regard to your own travel plans; the world would be full of great spaghetti dishes.

This chapter will help you in your quest to change it up by starting to perfect what you have. Use it as a guide, and then venture later into deeper waters. Have fun and believe that every detour could be a pathway into a new creation. Enjoying spaghetti, like great lovemaking, should be done again and again and again and again…

FRESH TOMATO MARINARA

A simple recipe can make all the difference. Use only the freshest tomatoes in this marinara. If I cannot find the best, I don't attempt this recipe. If good stuff goes in, love comes out.

Difficulty: 2

Makes: 2 quarts

10 tomatoes, vine-ripened
1½ Vidalia onions, medium
3 oz celery, diced small
2½ Tbsp garlic
¼ cup basil, chopped
1 oz parsley, chopped
¼ cup oregano, chopped
2 cups water
1 cup white wine
1 tsp coarse black pepper
1 Tbsp kosher sea salt

medium stock pot

Prep:

Place oil in bottom of stock pot. Turn stove top heat to medium. Add diced onions and celery. Sauté until translucent then add chopped garlic, fresh herbs, and white wine. Cook for 5 minutes, cooking off alcohol content.

Place in chopped tomatoes. Bring to a simmer. Pour in water and bring to a rolling simmer. Simmer for 10 minutes.

Remove from heat and salt and pepper, to taste.

When cool, place in blender and pulse until a chunky sauce consistency appears.

CRAWFISH MAC AND CHEESE

A New Orleans twist to an American classic, Mac and Cheese, has become all the rage in fine dining establishments. They even incorporate lobster or shrimp. We developed this recipe for common folk, like myself.

Difficulty: 2

Serves: 12

16 oz spiral pasta
1½ cup crawfish tail meat
3 whole eggs
2 cups milk
2 cups mixed cheese (cheddar, Monterey Jack, American)
½ cup parmesan cheese
1 Tbsp Old Bay Seasoning
2 tsp black pepper
1 tsp kosher sea salt
1 tsp seasoning salt
2 tsp dried parsley
4 oz butter
1 cup Panko breadcrumbs

medium stock pot
medium baking dish
small sauté pan

Prep:

Topping:
Melt butter in microwave and pour into bowl with Panko crumbs. Add parmesan cheese and set aside until needed.

Pasta:
Heat enough water in medium sauce pan to cook spiral pasta. Add salt and one teaspoon of olive oil. When water comes to simmer, place spiral pasta in water and cook until tender. Drain hot water from pasta and leave pasta in sauce pan. Fold in butter. Add cheese, cilantro, chopped garlic, sour cream, and milk. Mix well and pour into baking dish.

.

Crawfish:
In small sauté pan, add remaining olive oil. Carefully and quickly sauté crawfish. Place seasoned crawfish on top of pasta. Mix in with spoon. Cover with foil and cook for 35 minutes.

Remove foil and top with buttered breadcrumbs. Cook uncovered for additional 15 minutes, until bubbly and brown.

Serve hot from pan and receive the praise.

MOZZARELLA RAVIOLI WITH SPICY SAUSAGE

One of my favorite pasta dishes is simple ravioli. Growing up in South Philadelphia, Italian meats from 9th Street Market were the highlight of many a great dish.

Difficulty: 1

Serves: 4

Prep:

32 medium fresh mozzarella ravioli
Tip: I prefer a fresh product over a frozen one.
ice water (to cool pasta)
olive oil
2 tsp kosher sea salt
⅓ cup fresh basil, sliced
grated parmesan cheese

Fill medium stock pot with water. Add olive oil and kosher sea salt and bring to a boil over high heat on stove top.

Remove pasta from package set aside and wait until water comes to a boil.

Make an ice bath to cool off ravioli.

3 cups fresh marinara
10 oz spicy sausage, cut and fully cooked, then fold into marinara

Place ravioli in boiling water. When the ravioli began to float, remove from water and place in ice water to cool immediately.

medium stock pot
sauce pan

Heat spicy sausage marinara in sauce pan. Place ravioli in heated sauce.

Serve in flat pasta plate.

Top with grated cheese and fresh basil.

Serve with garlic bread or side salad.

SAFFRON MUSSELS

The key to this exciting recipe is using the freshest possible products you can find. Mussels should be odor-free and tightly closed. Discard any open mussels and have plenty of crusty bread on hand for the delicious broth that will remain at the bottom of the bowl.

Difficulty: 2

Serves: 4

1 large bag mussels, medium
2 cups cooked orzo pasta
¾ cup dry white wine
2 oz extra virgin olive oil
½ cup unsalted butter
⅓ cup chopped onion
⅓ cup chopped celery
1 tsp red pepper flake
2 oz fresh parsley
2 oz chopped garlic
2 cups water
salt and pepper

medium stock pot
shallow soup dish

Prep:

Clean mussels in warm water with salt to aid in eliminating debris. Also remove any bearded membranes.

In medium stock pot, add oil, onions, and celery.
Bring to simmer on medium heat.
When translucent, add garlic and red pepper flake. When garlic is golden in color, add white wine. Then, add parsley and butter.

Slowly add mussels and water. Cover the mussels with lid and turn down heat. Let simmer until the mussels open. Let stand for 5 minutes. Remove from heat.

Salt and pepper, to taste.

Arrange:

In a shallow soup dish or pasta bowl, place cooked orzo pasta in middle of bowl.

Arrange 10 mussels on the outside of pasta.

Ladle in broth as well as onion, celery, and chopped garlic.

Top with crusted bread and fresh parsley.

Enjoy!

SPINACH FETTUCCINE ALFREDO

I simply adore vegetable enriched pasta. Add roasted Holland peppers as a garnish and fresh crispy spinach to show off just a bit.

Difficulty: 2

Serves: 2

16 oz spinach fettuccine pasta
2 oz olive oil
water
2 tsp kosher sea salt

1 large roasted pepper
1 cup crispy spinach
⅓ cup parmesan cheese

Alfredo Sauce:
½ cup heavy cream
1 cup grated parmesan cheese
¼ cup roasted garlic
1 tsp red pepper flake
2 tsp kosher salt
2 tsp dried thyme
2 Tbsp olive oil
3 cups chicken or vegetable stock

medium stock pot
medium sauce pan
small sauce pan
bowl

Prep:

Fill medium stock pot with water. Add olive oil and kosher sea salt. Bring to a boil on stove over high heat.

Remove pasta from box and carefully place in boiling water. Stir when pasta collapses in water and stir on occasion, ensuring the pasta cooks evenly.

When pasta is cooked, remove and rinse with warm water to cool down. Place oil in bowl to coat pasta until needed.

Alfredo Sauce:
In medium sauce pan, heat olive oil on stove top.
Add garlic, sauté and quickly add stock, cheese and heavy cream. Bring to simmer, adding red pepper flake and thyme. Add black pepper, kosher salt and thicken with roux.

Place heated spinach fettuccine on plate.
Top with sauce, roasted red peppers, and crispy spinach.

Roasting Peppers:
If you have a gas stove, you are in good standing. Turn on burner and set pepper directly on flame, charring skin of pepper. Remove from flame when completely black.

Cover with foil and steam pepper for 10 minutes. Remove foil and carefully remove charred skin. Quickly rinse pepper.
Remove pit from pepper. Place pepper on cutting board and cut into strips. Garnish pasta with peppers and top with crispy spinach.

Crispy Spinach:
In small sauce pan, place cup of olive oil in pan and heat. When hot, place spinach in grease and cook until crispy. Remove from oil. Cover plate with paper towel and drain on paper-toweled plate. Sprinkle with parmesan cheese.

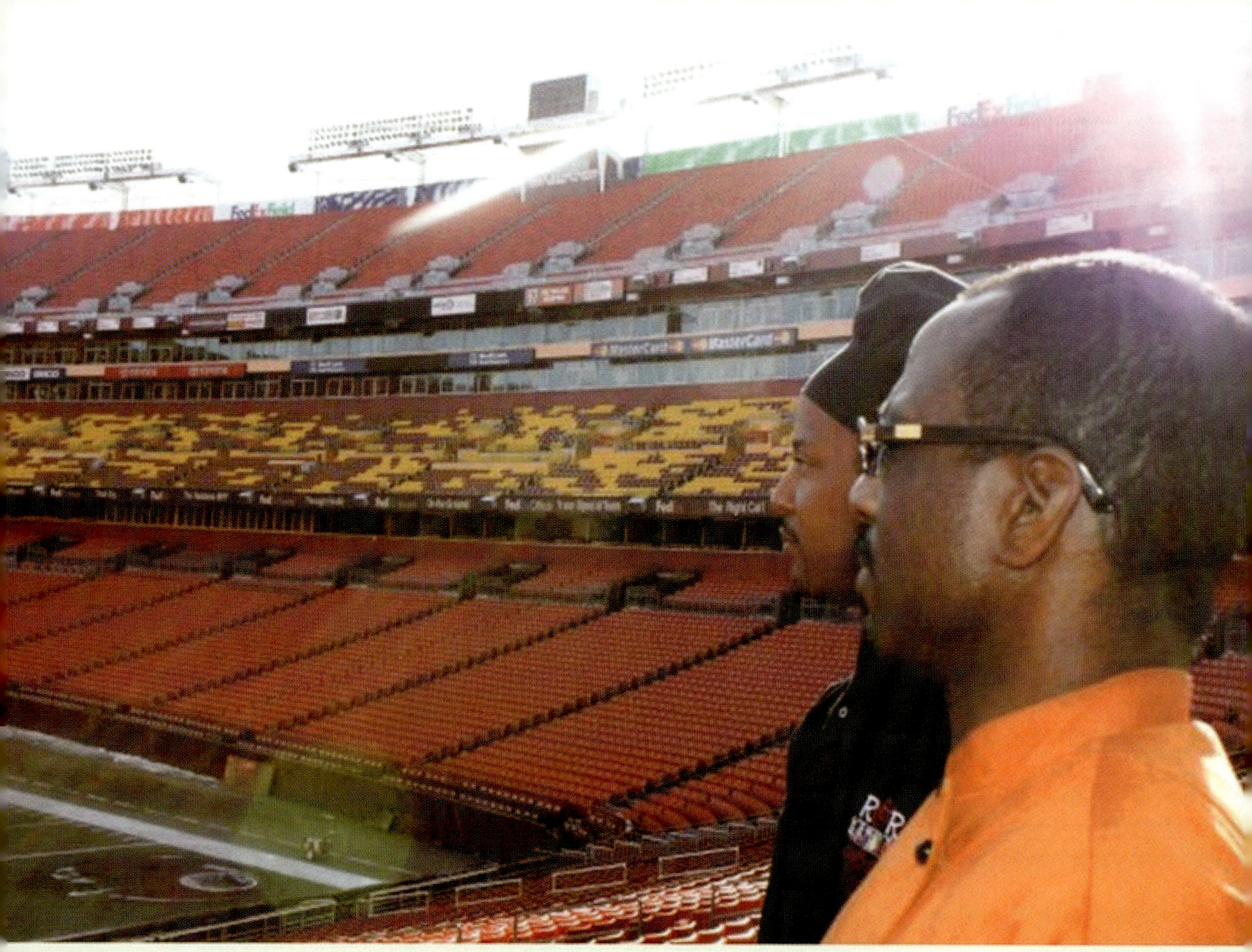
MasterCard
MasterCard

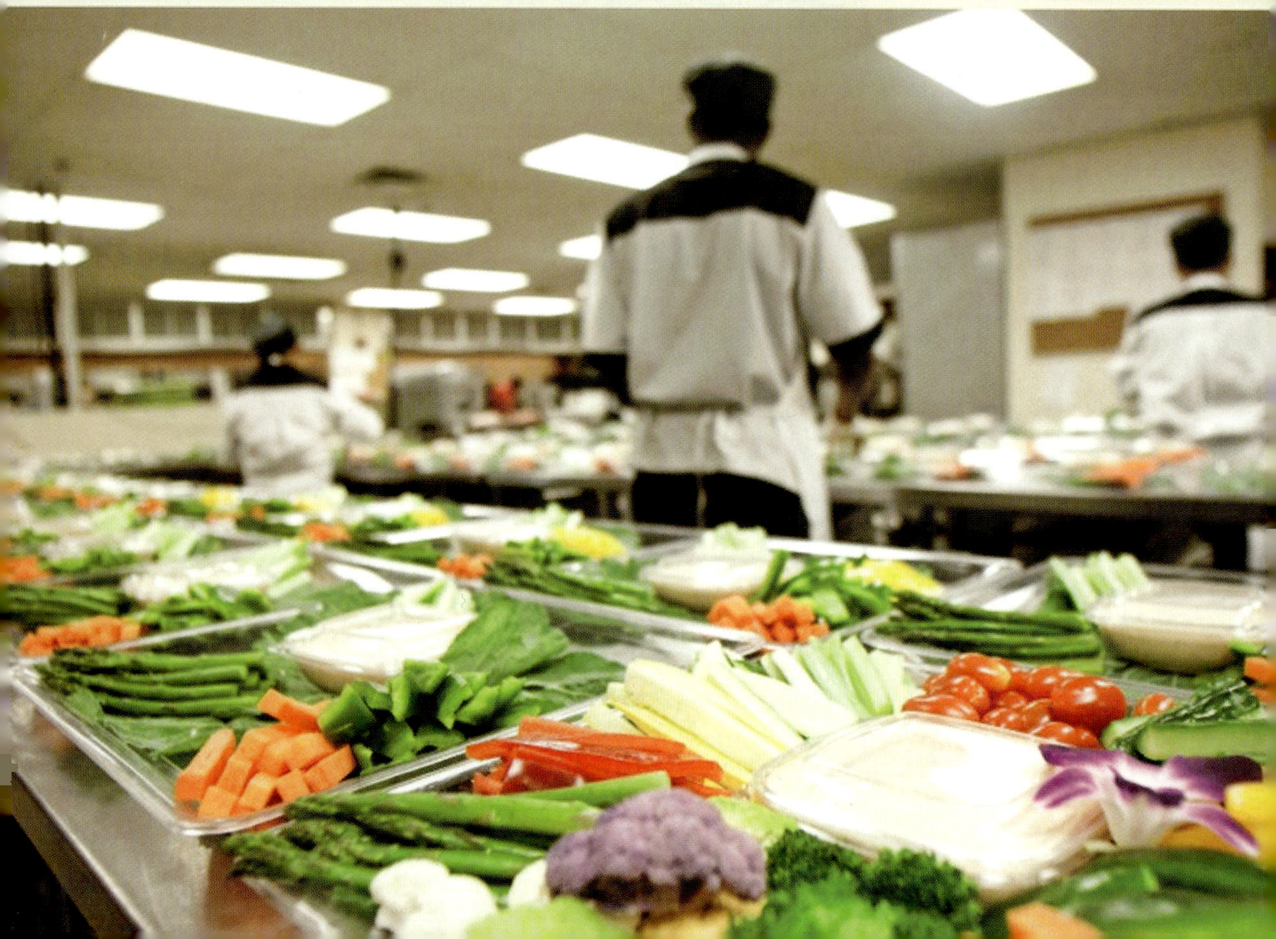

JERSEY SHORE CLAMS AND LINGUINE

One of my favorite late-night spots to get food is an Italian place in Atlantic City. You also never know who you may run into.

Difficulty: 2

Serves: 2

12 clams, whole
2 cups clams, chopped in juice
1 white onion, diced small
1 Tbsp scallions
1 Tbsp garlic
½ tsp red pepper flake
1½ cups white wine, dry
½ cup butter, unsalted
1 Tbsp parsley
⅓ cup parmesan cheese
12 oz linguine pasta
olive oil

medium stock pot
medium sauté pan
bowl

Prep:

In sink, rinse whole clams and set aside until needed. Open chopped clams and reserve juice in bowl.

In medium sauce pan, add olive oil. When heated, add chopped onions, garlic, red pepper flake, and fresh herbs.

Pour in white wine and bring to a simmer. Reduce for 2 minutes and add fresh clams along with reserved clams and juice. When clams open, add chopped clams and unsalted butter. Remove from heat and keep in sauce pan until needed.

Fill medium sauce pan halfway with salted water and one teaspoon of olive oil. Bring water to boil and add linguine pasta. Quickly stir, ensuring that the pasta does not stick together.

When pasta is cooked, carefully drain hot water and rinse with warm water. Place one tablespoon of olive oil in pasta and place in bowl with about 6 oz of pasta.

Ladle heated clam broth and chopped clams. Garnish with whole clams. Serve with crusted bread to enjoy clam broth. Sprinkle with parmesan cheese. Enjoy!

SPICY GROUND TURKEY SAUSAGE LASAGNA

A great way to utilize ground turkey and turkey sausage is to layer them between lasagna noodles and herb ricotta cheese. You can substitute seafood or beef, and pork seasoning also works well.

Difficulty: 3

Serves: 12

2 boxes lasagna noodles, cooked and laid flat on baking sheet
10 oz turkey sausage, chopped and cooked
1 lb ground turkey
1 small white onion
2 Tbsp chopped garlic
2 cups ricotta cheese
4 whole eggs
1 cup parmesan cheese
2 Tbsp fresh parsley
2 tsp red pepper flake
2 tsp garlic powder
1 Tbsp ground thyme
⅓ cup fresh basil
2 cups mozzarella cheese
8 oz sliced smoked provolone
3 cups Marinara (See recipe on page 100.)

medium stock pot
large baking dish

Prep:

Sausage and Ground Turkey:
In medium sauté pan, add olive oil. Heat on high heat. Place ground turkey and sausage in sauté pan. Add chopped garlic, thyme, and 1 tsp red pepper flake. Cook until done. Remove from heat. Drain liquid and discard. Reserve meat until assembly.

Ricotta Mixture:
Mix ricotta, eggs, parmesan cheese, thyme, red pepper flake, parsley, and black pepper. Reserve until assembly.
Place oil in bottom of baking dish. Sprinkle with parmesan cheese. Ladle thin coat of fresh marinara on bottom of baking dish. Lay pasta sheet, covering sauce on bottom of baking dish.

Scoop teaspoon balls of ricotta cheese mixture, evenly spacing 10 of them on bottom. Sprinkle ground turkey sausage mixture. Top with mixed cheese, blend cheese, and then smoked provolone. Ladle fresh marinara on top of smoked provolone. Top with pasta, placing them across previous direction of pasta on bottom of baking dish. Repeat process. Depending on how deep your baking dish is, try and complete four layers.

Preheat oven to 350 degrees.
When the top layer is finished, spread thin coat of fresh marinara on top and a layer of smoked provolone and mozzarella cheese. Cover with wrap and then foil. Place in preheated oven. Cook for 1 hour. Remove foil and finish cooking for 10 minutes.

It's certainly true that this dish gets better each day it's left in the refrigerator.

106

ASIAN VEGETABLE SOBA NOODLES

Asian flavors, mixed vegetables, a hint of Soy, fresh Soba noodles, and fresh ginger.

Difficulty: 1

Serves: 4

½ cup snow peas, trimmed
½ cup broccoli
¼ cup carrot sticks
¼ cup celery
¼ cup mushroom
¼ cup baby corn
¼ cup green onions
2 Tbsp cilantro
1 tsp ginger
½ tsp red pepper flake
¼ cup rice wine vinegar
¼ cup sesame oil
1 Tbsp olive oil
12 oz soba noodles, cooked

medium sauté pan

Prep:

In medium sauté pan, pour in olive oil. Place heat to high. Add chopped ginger, celery, and mushrooms. Begin to sauté.

Place remaining vegetables in sauté pan and season with garlic. Pour in rice wine vinegar and sesame oil.

Add cooked soba noodles and red pepper flake. Cover with vegetable stock. Reduce by half and add fresh cilantro. Sprinkle with sesame seeds.

Serve with chopsticks and sake.

When women speak out,
do we listen?

I. Love

II. Trust

III. Intimacy

IV. Communication

These are the four pillars
of a woman's relationship foundation.

Quality Time Equals a Quality Relationship.

Spending time together means
more to me than any store-bought gift.

A Woman's Heart: *What personal values must a partner have to conquer your heart?*

Ladies: *I've always been called a "daddy's girl" and it's a title that I've always accepted. My dad is my number one man, my rock, my strength and his family was and always has been his number-one priority. I've always said I won't settle until I find a man with those same values. My dad served 4 tours of duty during the Vietnam War and is a Purple Heart recipient. He met and married my mother while he was stationed in Thailand, and he brought her back to the United States at the end of his service in the U.S. Army. Their journey hasn't been a perfect one, but it's one that's stood the test of time. During the most crucial times and more than 40 years, 4 children, 9 grandchildren, and 1 great-grandson later, they are still happily married.*

While dad may have disapproved of a lot of things in my life, he always supported everything I did 100 percent. Besides telling me he loves me on a regular basis, my dad is the only man who has ever made me feel genuinely beautiful without expecting something in return. I know on the rare days when I'm visiting my parent's house and I actually put effort into my appearance, my dad will tell me something to the effect of, "Angela, you belong on the cover of Essence magazine." And even when I don't believe it's true myself, I know he does.

But what I love most about my dad, and want a man in my love life to imitate, is that through all of the tragedies and successes my family has gone through, he's never wavered in his passion for his family. He's a wonderful provider. He understands me and doesn't judge me. After raising 3 girls; he's a forgiving man and knows how to sit back and let us find our way, without stepping in to intervene. My dad is book-smart, street-smart, patient, unconditionally loving, generous, joyful, carefree, and witty. But most of all, what I love about my father, is his tenderness and wisdom. Wisdom that comes from his years of drive, and his ability to provide for his family and leading the way he has. So, in my partner, I would want the same personal values that my dad has and I thank him for showing me how a real man can love unconditionally.

Thanks Dad, for everything. Thanks for being the best, because even though you set the bar real high, and I joke that it may be somehow damaging, I know it's not, and I know it'll be worth it in the end. You've taught me to never, ever settle. Lucky me to have a dad like you. ~Angela Green~

A Woman's Heart: Do partners usually know what women like and dislike sexually?

Ladies: *I believe they do not know because every person is different. Therefore, as a woman, I have to let my partner know what I want sexually.*

Ladies: *Sexually, I feel men think we are all the same, but we are each unique like our bodies and sexual desires. A bite of exploration is okay when we first begin to be intimate. As things progress, the conversation should happen unless he is just an amazing and giving lover.*

Ladies: *We have been conditioned to except whatever he brings to the sexual table. If I am not a fan of what is on my plate, I usually don't bother to eat it... Hint, Hint!*

A Woman's Heart: *How do you let your partner know your intimate desires?*

Ladies: *Its hard, I have been trying to approach this subject in my relationship for a while now. I feel like I may never be able to talk openly with him. I smile as if all is well, but I so need him to hear me roar!*

Ladies: *I simply tell him. We both know we have had past encounters. I am in love with my man, so our passionate and intimate relationship is an extension of how much I love him. So, the same way I tell him I love him, I communicate that in our non-verbal communication.*

Ladies: *Is there a way to tell a man, that it does not work for me sexually? If so, I need that book!* ~Anonymous, California

Ladies: *Have fun with it; take control every now and then. Let him be the man, but really show how HE can be the MAN!* ~Cookie Washington~

A woman's Heart: *How important is your partner's physical attributes?*

Ladies: *Physical attraction is what attracts people to each other initially. I think that once you get to know a person on the inside, physical attributes are not as important. However, I think it's important to keep myself up for my partner.*

Ladies: *We spend so much time and some painful moments pleasing the sight of man and the world we live in as women. The least my partner can do is keep up his appearance. Men have it so easy!*

Ladies: He is my baby and my life, so I aid in his appearance by selecting flattering things for him to wear when we go out. I also try and hint occasionally if I see him in the kitchen late nights. I remedy that by keeping my baby in the bedroom at nights. I become his late-night, early-morning snack.

Ladies: *I love my husband for who he is on the inside. I drool over my husband for his strong hands and broad shoulders. His ability to calm me down with a teddy-bear-like hug, but his strength I need when it's just one of those nights; I need him to come get me because I have been bad!*

A Woman's Heart: *How important is your partner's relationships with other woman?*
Ladies: It depends on the relationship. If it is a professional relationship, then it is not a problem. I don't have a problem with my partner's relationships with women because he makes me feel secure.

110

Ladies: *I am and always will trust my man until he gives me reason to challenge that. To be honest women have become the enemy in many relationships. If you know he has a wife, woman, or girlfriend do not lower your standards and become the side chick. What have we reduced ourselves to accepting from men?*

Ladies: *I am and every woman should be there partners' best friend. If there are any female friends they should go through you to get to him. Cheating people are going to cheat, so what is a girl to do?*

NOURISHMENT WHILE BEING NOURISHED

Food often tames the emotional core of all our relationships.
Food, like any great lover, is to be savored, enjoyed, and treasured.

Ever been sick and weak in the inner parts of your body and spirit? Being a diabetic, I have often experienced the highs and lows of being drained emotionally and physically. I frequently work longer hours than I need to. I invest a great deal of emotional energy in trying to understand clients and food trends. All these things pile up on me like excess baggage. They are burdens that are like the spoiled parts of great meals. They tend to be the fatty parts of the steak that should have been removed prior to service. We all tend to take doggie bags home from restaurants because we don't want to throw away food. We say people are starving somewhere. And yet the doggie bags stay in our cooler growing mold because of our great emotional intentions.

As we consider the nourishment of the body and the soul, we have to be careful that we are not fooled. The body oftentimes gives off a false sense of new health. There are times when you feel the need to work in solitude because your body is under duress. In a swoop of false security you get your second wind. And you're out the door without getting the proper rest and nourishment that your body is craving.

The same will and can happen in the process of preparing a meal. At times, we think we can take short cuts that may not be seen or discovered. The frightening thing is that it can be masked for a moment but in the end, and probably at the least opportune time, the secret will come.

Nourishment means more than feeding; it's more than a full belly. To be nourished is to be revived, to be relieved of what ails you, to be released from the toxic thoughts and duress of the body by placing it in a better environment. The process is not one that is easily rushed. Careful planning has to be employed when thinking of nourishment. If someone places their heart in your hand, be honest and make evaluations as if it were your heart in your hands. Is the heart in good hands? There are so many people that are sick with emotional food poisoning. It looked good at first; it even tasted okay. It was within the allotted perishing date, yet in seventy-two hours they are asking the doctors what the heck hit them. Anyone that has experienced food poisoning knows that it takes time for the toxins to run their course and get out of the system. I'm not talking about the twenty-four hour bug. It's when you open yourself up to that great meal and it turns out to be the most deplorable thing you ever experienced. All of us have gotten hurt by winter tomatoes to some degree.

True nourishment is the antidote; it has the ability to make one better. It has the ability to remove past aches and to exhume and discard past hurts and tired conversations, the ability to make you forget past hurts. When you are reintroduced to the very thing that laid you out flat on your back and given the opportunity to engage in a meal—still with apprehension—to be given the right product, just the way you ordered it and to still be standing after seventy-two hours, that's restoration of faith in that thing. That's nourishment.

My passion for food seems to always drive me to places that go far beyond feeding the masses. I want to feed places that common menu items can't satisfy. I want to be the restorer of lost faith—faith that was lost because of chefs that complicate food and disguise the food's God-given attributes. The Chef Mike Experience is about the business of nourishment. There are plenty of great chefs but they sometimes fall out of love with the center of the plates and grow indifferent to the silent roar of the consumer.

It's a great gift. Your staff can't create your food art and unique flavor or rethink the process. That same consumer is watching you on television and they go to dine because of the sizzle that is associated with your products. Just nourish the people. We have been charged with a great responsibility to feed the masses, keep them healthy and always try and keep them in the center of our minds. In the event that we fail them, it's back to Hamburger Helper.

I take my profession very seriously. I nourish my guests, my fan base. I enjoy the empty plate and the silent thank you they show by rubbing their belly. The nourishment aspect of cooking is alive and well in the Chef Mike Experience. I will continue to make recipes that provide you Nourishment while being Nourished—you can count on that!

Please be careful not to make false advertisements in cooking or love. Give what you want in return. Love like you have never been hurt and cook like you're feeding an ailing friend. Food has healing powers that are so underrated. But the body knows best.

SMOTHERED BONE-ON PORK CHOPS

On occasion, I just can't resist the urge for some good pork chops deep fried and smothered in gravy. Pro-Bowl Corner Back De'Angelo Hall staples during off season. His family is such a joy to work with.

Difficult: 2

Serves: 4

Prep:

6 Pork Chops
1 Onion, medium sliced
1 tsp garlic, chopped
2 cups Flour
1 tsp Coarse black pepper
2 oz Texas Hot Sauce
2 oz Worchester Sauce
2 cups Chicken or Beef Stock.
vegetable oil

large sauté pan
bowl

Rinse Pork chops and place on large plate.
On a separate plate pour flour, seasoning salt, black pepper, garlic powder, and parsley. Mix all ingredients.
In separate bowl mix whole eggs, hot sauce, and water, mixing until incorporated.
In large sauté pan add vegetable oil and began to heat carefully on high heat. While oil is heating up begin coating Pork Chops. Submerge Pork Chops in seasoned egg wash for 10 minutes. Remove each pork chop and lay on floured plate. Dredge bone in pork chops coating each side. Continue process until all chops are floured.

Administer fry ready test. When oil is hot, shake off excess flour from pork chops. Carefully place in oil. Cook until golden-brown and then carefully turn chops over. Lower your heat so that the grease will stay at a great fry temperature but not burn. When chops are cooked place on draining plate. Cook all Pork chops and turn down heat.
Drain most of renderings into another pan. Place sauté pan back over medium heat. There should be ⅓ cup of grease you cooked pork chops in. Toss in sliced onions and quickly sauté. Add chopped garlic and parsley. Sprinkle in 2 Tbsp of flour and mix through onions and garlic mixture. Slowly add chicken or beef stock. Whisk until thickened and add 2 oz of Worchester Sauce. Whisk in sauté pan and bring to a simmer.

Place pork chops in gravy and allow to simmer, coating the pork chops. Heat through and remove from heat. Serve with your favorite sides.

ROUX (QUICK VERSION)

If you need to thicken sauce or soups, roux can be your best ally in the kitchen. I generally keep a few ounces on hand just in case I need to thicken up a sauce or soup. The longer you keep it in pan, the darker the roast.

Difficulty: 1

Serves:

Prep:

¾ cup butter, unsalted
½ cup flour
½ tsp seasoning salt

small sauté pan

Place heat on low. In small sauté pan, slowly melt butter and add seasoning salt. Allow butter to caramelize and quickly add flour. Stir to incorporate, and cook through, scraping from sides until desired color.

Remove and put in cooling container.

Set aside until needed.

Cover and refrigerate for prolonged use.

CRAWFISH ÉTOUFFÉE

The flavors of New Orleans characterize some of my most seductive dinners. The warming spices, roux, and gravies allow you to take a culinary vacation in your very own kitchen. You may have to actually travel for great beignets, though.

Difficulty: 2

Serves: 4

2 lbs crawfish
1 onion, medium-diced
½ cup celery
⅓ cup Holland pepper, small-diced
2 tsp garlic, chopped
¼ cup scallions, sliced
½ cup tomato, diced in juice
1 Tbsp Roux (See recipe on page 117.)
3 cups seafood stock or chicken stock
1Tbsp Old Bay Seasoning
2 oz fresh parsley
2 tsp chili powder
1 tsp black pepper
2 cups long-grain rice
1 oz vinegar
1 Tbsp thyme, dried

large sauté pan
small sauce pan for rice

Prep:

Rice:
On stove top, place 2 cups of water in small sauce pan. Pour in one capful of vinegar. Add dried thyme. Pour in 1 ½ cups of rice to liquid. Bring to a boil over high heat, reduce to a simmer, and cover. Cook until water evaporates and remove from stove top. Rice should be tender to the bite and not sticky.

In medium sauté pan, add olive oil. Place on medium heat. Add onions, celery, and Holland peppers. Sauté until tender.

Add crawfish tail meat, garlic, scallions, chili powder, Old Bay Seasoning, and roux. Incorporate and then add half of seafood stock. Mix to incorporate, add remaining stock. Bring to simmer for 15 minutes. On low simmer, add more stock if you desire a thin consistency.

In large plate, place 4 oz of rice on center of plate. Ladle hot Crawfish Étouffée over top.

Serve with sliver queen corn bread

LAMB SLIDERS WITH CRANBERRY MAYO

An amazing snack for parties or business mixers. The sweet tasting lamb is accented by tart and creamy cranberry mayo.

Difficulty: 1

Serves: 8

5 lbs ground lamb
4 oz white onions, minced
1 Tbsp chervil
2 tsp cilantro
2 tsp coriander
1 Tbsp kosher sea salt
1 Tbsp black pepper
25 potato slider buns
arugula (baby)
fresh Roma tomato, sliced

Cranberry Mayo (See recipe on page 30.)

medium sauté pan
large mixing bowl

Note: Preferred method of cooking is grilled.

Preparation:

In large mixing bowl, combine ground lamb and minced onions. Add fresh herbs, black pepper, and kosher sea salt. Mix to incorporate flavors.
Form into 3-oz patties and set aside.

Heat outdoor grill and season grates with olive oil.
When grill is heated, place sliders on top.
While sliders are cooking, arrange potato rolls on plate. Spread bottom with Cranberry Mayo.

When sliders are cooked to desired temperature, place slider on bun. Top with baby arugula and a slice of Roma tomato.

Serve to guests as a standalone appetizer or combine with fresh fries.

BEER BATTER ONION RINGS

Great in every way, these large sweet Vidalia onions are dipped and fried in a sweetened lager batter. Serve with spicy ketchup or malt vinegar. What a tasty golden snack!

Difficulty: 3

Serves: 6

Prep:

3 large onions, cut into rings
1 egg
¾ cup flour
4 oz lager beer
1 Tbsp garlic pepper
3 oz Panko breadcrumbs
water (chilled with ice)
4 cups vegetable oil

medium stock pot
bowl

Place cut onion rings in chilled ice water. Let soak for 20 minutes.

Mix whole egg with lager beer, flour (2 oz), and breadcrumbs (3 oz). Set aside until needed.

Place flour (4 oz) and garlic pepper (1 Tbsp) in a separate bowl.

When onion rings have soaked for twenty minutes, remove from chilled water and place in seasoned flour. Be careful not to break up rings and make sure they are evenly coated with flour.

When finished coating rings in flour, start preheating vegetable oil in medium stock pot.

When grease has passed the fry ready test, carefully dip onion rings in beer batter. Remove excess and carefully place in heated grease. Onion rings will eventually float. Use fork to turn over onion rings, cooking them until golden-brown on each side. Remove from hot vegetable oil and drain on plate layered with paper towel. Sprinkle with kosher sea salt.

Serve with favorite dipping sauce or add to any steak dinner for an excellent WOW flavor factor.

CALF LIVER SMOTHERED IN SWEET ONION GRAVY

On occasion, my table would be set with an amazing rich deep red wine, buttery rolls, and candles. And for the main course, crispy tender liver in a red wine scented gravy with caramelized onions. I would be the first at the table. Reminding me of my childhood favorite.

Difficulty :1

Serves : 2

1 lb calf liver
½ cup onions white, sliced
½ cup red wine, full bodied
¾ cup beef stock
½ cup flour
2 tsp ground black pepper
2 tsp kosher salt
1 tsp chopped garlic
2 tsp thyme, dried
⅓ cup olive oil

Prep:

Clean liver by rinsing and removing course membranes.
Place on clean plate and add salt and pepper.

In separate plate, add flour and dried thyme.

Place medium sauté pan on stove top on medium heat. Add olive oil and heat.

When oil is hot enough to pass fry test:
Dredge seasoned liver in seasoned flour.
Carefully place liver in heated olive oil.
Quickly cook on both sides until golden-brown.
Sprinkle 1 Tbsp flour in sauté pan.
Stir and add red wine.
Add beef stock and stir until gravy is smooth.

Allow gravy to cook for 10 minutes with liver still in sauté pan.

Remove from heat and serve alongside short-grain rice or savory mashed potatoes.

Don't forget to have a glass of wine for yourself.

GROUND BISON MEATLOAF WITH CREMINI MUSHROOM GRAVY

When my athlete clients return to full training status, I only cook lean meats for them to consume. They love home-style cooking, and meatloaf is a client favorite. We use ground bison and infuse fresh herbs and sauces to enhance flavor profile.

Difficulty: 2

Serves: 8

3 lbs ground bison
1 small onion, minced
⅓ cup celery, minced
4 tsp garlic, chopped
1 oz parsley
2 oz thyme
½ cup tomato sauce
3 whole eggs
3 Tbsp Panko breadcrumbs
2 oz parmesan cheese
3oz green bell pepper, minced

meatloaf pan

Gravy:
2 oz olive oil
4 oz cremini mushrooms
2 oz celery
2 oz onions
1½ tsp garlic
3 oz beef stock
5 oz chicken stock
Roux (See recipe on page 117.)

medium sauté pan

Prep:

Preheat oven to 350 degrees.
Place olive oil on bottom of meat loaf pan. When evenly coated, drain excess oil and sprinkle breadcrumbs in bottom. Pour out excess crumbs. Set aside while you mix and form meatloaf.
In a large bowl, add ground bison and all diced vegetables. Place in parmesan cheese, fresh herbs, finally adding eggs. Mix to incorporate all ingredients. Slowly pour in tomato sauce. Mix to incorporate.
Turn seasoned meat into loaf pan and form to fit mold. Place a layer of tomato sauce over bison meatloaf. Cover with foil and place in preheated oven for 5 minutes or until internal temperature reaches 155 degrees.
Remove loaf from oven and allow to cool for 10 minutes. Place knife along edges then carefully remove loaf from pan onto cutting board.
Cut loaf into one-inch slices. Place one slice of meatloaf per serving plate. Ladle mushroom gravy (see below) over top with some saluted cremini mushrooms.
Serve with a classic starch and vegetable. Makes you always feel closer to home.

Mushroom Gravy:
In medium sauté pan add olive oil. Place onions, garlic, celery, and mushrooms in pan. Sauté until onions are translucent. Pour in Worcestershire sauce, flour, and parsley in pan. Stir in flour ,then pour in chicken and beef stock. Stir until smooth. Let reduce until desired thickness.

SPINACH WITH CRISPY GARLIC CHIPS

My mother Cynthia Stevenson instilled in me our body's need for green vegetables in our diet. Although some of my NFL clients know they need them, they sometimes shy away from them. So my challenge (which I welcome) is to create recipes that change their views on eating vegetables.

Difficulty: 1

Serves: 2

24 oz spinach
3 oz red onion
5 cloves garlic, thinly sliced
3 oz olive oil
2 oz soy sauce
½ tsp red pepper flake
1 Tbsp Smart Blend Spread

large sauté pan
small sauté pan

Prep:

Preheat large sauté pan.

Place olive oil in sauté pan. Quickly add chopped fresh spinach. Spinach will shrink instantly. Continue adding until halfway cooked. Add red onions and soy sauce. Sprinkle in red pepper flake.

Garlic Prep:
In small sauté pan, heat olive oil.

Slice garlic cloves thin. When oil is hot, remove from heat and place in garlic slices.

Cook quickly, then remove the crispy garlic chips. Sprinkle chips with salt and reserve for garnish atop of spinach.

CHILEAN SEA BASS IN SMOKED TOMATO SAUCE

An amazing flavor packed fish. It is on the higher end in price when purchasing fish, but well worth the price. Pairing this flaky fish with a subtle smoky tomato broth is a culinary delight and sure to dazzle your guest.

Difficulty: 2

Serves: 4

Prep:

4 (5-oz) Chilean sea bass filets
4 whole garlic
¼ cup fresh chervil
1 Tbsp adobo chipotle pepper paste
1 cup tomatoes with juice
¾ cup vegetable stock
¼ cup celery
¼ cup green onions
½ cup Panko breadcrumbs
2 oz olive oil
½ cup dry white wine
1 Tbsp butter

Place medium sauté pan on stove top.
Place olive oil and turn heat to medium.
Rinse sea bass filets, then sprinkle with salt and pepper.
Top with Panko crumbs.

When oil is heated, quickly sear sea bass, Panko side down, to a golden-brown.

Remove from sauté pan and set aside.

Place sauté pan back on stove top on medium heat.
Add whole garlic, adobo paste, and white wine.
Place tomatoes in sauté pan and cook for 10 minutes.

Add fresh chervil and vegetable stock.
Continue to cook, reducing by half.

Preheat oven to 350 degrees.

Place seared Chilean sea bass in baking dish.
Pour smoky tomato sauce in baking dish.
Add butter and green onions.
Cook uncovered in preheated oven for 15 minutes.
Carefully remove fish.
Ladle sauce over fish and serve alongside your favorite vegetables or small pasta.

SPINACH RICOTTA CHEESE GNOCCHI WITH
GARLIC CREAM SAUCE

In South Philadelphia, I would travel with my mother to the Italian market. We would sometimes have a small tasting of pasta, sausage, and even cheese. But the fondest treat was these amazing pillows.

Difficulty: 3

Serves: 4

1 lb potato (Yukon Gold)
3 oz spinach
3 oz ricotta cheese
1 cup flour
1 egg
1 tsp salt
3 tsp garlic
2 tsp pepper
1 cup heavy cream
2 oz basil, chopped
1½ cups vegetable stock
1 tsp red pepper flake
3 oz onion
2 oz olive oil
water
ice
Roux (See recipe on page 117.)

medium stock pot
medium sauté pan
2 large bowls

Prep:

Fill medium stock pot with water for cooking potatoes. Add salt. Peel and quarter potatoes and place in water. Cook until tender, drain water, and reserve.

In large bowl, place flour, chopped spinach, ricotta cheese, egg, 1 tsp garlic, and 1 tsp pepper. Mix all ingredients. Place dough in refrigerator and chill.

While dough is chilling, preheat medium sauté pan and add oil. Add minced white onions, vegetable stock, cream, chopped basil, and red pepper flake. Bring to simmer and add Roux. Sprinkle parmesan cheese and remove from heat.

When dough is firm, cut into half-inch strips. Roll like play dough, then cut into half-inch pieces. Freeze until needed..

When water boils, add gnocchi in water. Fill separate bowl with ice and water, this will cool down gnocchi. When gnocchi floats, remove from hot water and carefully place in ice bath. When chilled, remove from ice bath and add salt. Heat garlic cream sauce in sauté pan. Place gnocchi in sauce and heat throughout. Place in bowl and top with grated cheese.

GOLDEN RAISIN AND SCALLION QUINOA

I was introduced to this grain by circumstance. Cooking it almost weekly has allowed me to study its chameleon like qualities and develop recipes with different spice profiles and still allow the subtle nuttiness of the grain to shine through. I have grown to love it and now keep a bag in my pantry at my home in Virginia.

Difficulty: 1

Serves: 4

Prep:

2 cups quinoa
3 oz celery, diced
3 oz scallions, chopped
4 oz golden raisins
1½ cups water
2 cups vegetable broth
2 Tbsp chervil
1½ tsp black pepper
kosher sea salt, to taste

medium stock pot
baking dish
bowl

In medium stock pot, place olive oil in preheated pan.
Pour in celery, scallion, and golden raisins.
Quickly sauté.
Deglaze with vegetable stock.
Add water and bring to simmer.
When liquid is to a rolling simmer, add quinoa.
Lower heat on stovetop. Allow to simmer for about twenty minutes until quinoa blooms and becomes full and tender.

Remove from stock pot and pour in baking dish,. There may be some reserved liquid.

Place in bowl and serve as a side dish, or add grilled vegetables for an amazing vegan lunch experience.

SPICE OF LIFE - VI

Nourishment

Feeding the Mind, Body, and Soul

*I know that I have the task of providing the nutritional needs in
order to nurture the mind, body, and soul of my family.
Therefore, I take pride in preparing meals.
I love to hear my husband say "I can taste the love in the food."
Intimacy in the kitchen leads to intimacy in the bedroom!*

The Heart is the Home in Which Loves Dwells

*The Heart is the Key to Love.
We must chase after God with our whole heart so that
He can give us the desires of our heart.
This, along with love, will help us to sustain our relationships.*

Women are Watching Our Actions Towards Others

*I LOVE a man who loves and cherishes his mother,
or that is how he will treat me.
A man with a servant's heart who won't hesitate
to help others tugs at MY heartstrings.*

A Woman's Heart: *What should a partner do get to know their woman?*

Ladies: *When a man sees women or acknowledges he's interested, he should let it be known. Many times women are standing by for the approach of a man.*

Ladies: *The old fashion ways of courting are not dead. So, if a connection is made and contact information is exchanged... A great way to have a women thinking of you as her main priority is to call her instead of texting. And this should be the first thing you do when you wake up, just for a quick "good morning" with some humorous banter and wish her a good day. Texting should start after you've spoken and made some verbal contact earlier. But texting is not for conversation because if you are both busy, some conversations can be had in a quick two-minute phone call. She would appreciate it more. Also, be the last voice she hears at night.*

Ladies: *Compliment her. If you like her hair, say so. You get her blushing for sure. Women want to hear how pretty she is more than how sexy she is. Descriptive words set you apart. Like "I love the way your hair moves when you walk!"*

Ladies: *If you're really interested, make sure she feels like she's a priority and not an option. Call her and ask her out on a date several days ahead; she would likely not turn you down. Be creative, go on a city tour, and walk in the park or billiards... Something that will be fun and entertaining, but yet light enough to spark conversation and see each other's personalities in non-threatening environments.*

Ladies: *During conversations, listen. Listening to her usually opens up opportunities to win her heart, especially when you show her you've been listening. Take advantage of opportunities to help. As an example, if you're listening, you'll know when trash day is. If you know she works late and her trash goes out on a particular day, ask her out for dinner and on those nights and offer to take out her trash for her when you pick her up.*

Ladies: *Be engaging and share your interests instead of relying on her on to ask all the questions, because men hate answering a bunch of questions. When asking about her interests, ask non-threatening questions, like, "What's on your bucket list?" or "What's the most adventure you've had?"*

A Woman's Heart: *What should a partner do get to know their woman?*

Ladies: *Take the time to find out what you both have in common and spend quality time doing things you both would enjoy. Take her around your friends and family and watch her interactions. Hang around her when she's doing things she loves, and kick it with her friends and family. You'll learn a lot, cook together, and play board games, just the two of you... Go to* *church together. Get to know one another's values, beliefs and what shapes them. Learn and share each other's passions and live them out!*

Ladies: *I forget what it feels like to be courted, and because of that, I am single. Most often, it's hard to be my authentic self because men's approach and pursuit is all about them. It has become a turn-off, and instead of spending my time with a man doing something fun, engaging in conversation, enjoying a meal or sharing intimate time together, I have to put my guards up and it puts them off, and because you have to set boundaries that don't have to be there if there was some genuine effort on their part. Dating has become a chore.* ~Vonetta Dumas

TILL DEATH DO US PART

Imagine life without the enchanting luscious foods of your childhood.
Imagine never having loved or been loved.
Imagine never placing your heart in harm's way.

Till death do us part. It has been recited by many married couples, yet only a few spouses actually experience the fulfillment of this monumental vow. Being without the object of your affection, without your childhood sweetheart, without the one who is the air beneath your wings is a chilling thought. Consider the person who has lost a lover and who has endured the ills wrought by loneliness, day after day, night after night. Memories of being together with their lover can invoke heartaches so fierce that they could never have been imagined—the yearning to hold and to be held, never to breath the aroma of their lover or savor the flavor that invoked timeless dreams. The bond between two people who really love each other is not easily severed.

In a similar way, I form a connection with great food. Whenever I come across a great food I take time to savor every moment, to utterly enjoy every nuance, every sensation, every discernible taste. I document every detail in my mind so that when I come upon a not-so-pleasant dish I can retreat to that magical place.

I would like to encourage you to do the same. Food is an expression to be analyzed. When most people dine, the stomach is usually the driving force. The next time you sit down to dine on a wonderful meal, instead of consuming the food to take care of your aching stomach, take time and think about what went into this wonderful meal. Someone's heart and soul went into the preparation of this creation. What emotional state were they in? What place in their life were they in? What story is the food telling you about hands that created it? Let's hope it is a good romance novel.

Some food items I have learned to love and some I am madly in love with. They placed me in a state of panic when I thought of this chapter. It brings me great joy to know that I've grown up on some of these foods and enjoyed them throughout my life. I feel very privileged to have a mother who helped shape my palate by introducing me to every type of food imaginable. The anticipation of every meal was the highlight of those days as a young chef prodigy in the making. She introduced me to ice cream that tasted of roasted pistachios and took me to places where the butter was so sweet that it tasted like candy. Experiences like these served to make very moment spent with her a timeless pleasure.

The recipes presented in this chapter are not entirely all mine. There are some chefs who helped me in this chapter, contributing their amazing creations. Having had the privilege of partaking in their fare has made me a better chef. I am a firm believer that if someone does it better than me, then by all means I will stand aside and let them do it. I am not going to try to outdo them. A chef's best meal is usually one that he or she doesn't cook.

Having consumed some of these meals has made me the chef that I am. Having experienced them has made me the richest man on the planet. Having been married has shown me that a man is to be with a woman. Having experienced a divorce has shown me the reasons why man is joined to woman. My life, with all its successes and failures, has prepared me to write this book. Great food is the standard by which not-so-great meals are measured. Poor service makes you pay premium prices because the service is guaranteed. We've all heard it said that the way to a man's hearts is through his stomach. Even a bad cook can tame the most discriminating food aficionado, but when a man sees the results of his woman's hands, he embraces her differences, her frailty, and the way God made woman and man. In her efforts, she grows in respect and confidence that even though she may not be the best cook in the world, she can make a sandwich, and put two pieces of cheese on it.

I am the richest man in the world because I live life expecting great things, I expect the good from people, and I have tapped into the world's deepest mystery:

The way to a woman's heart...

BBQ BLACK BEANS

Summer cookouts would be no fun without baked beans. I enjoy switching out black beans for a smoky flavorful side dish.

Difficulty: 2

Serves: 4

16 oz black beans (cooked, drained, and rinsed)
3 oz white onion, diced
3 oz celery, minced
1 Tbsp garlic, chopped
2 Tbsp cilantro
½ cup chili sauce
¾ cup ketchup
2 oz Liquid Smoke
3 oz brown sugar
⅓ cup Dijon mustard
2 oz olive oil
1 tsp chili powder

medium stock pot

Prep:

Preheat large stock pot. Place in olive oil.
Add onions, celery, and garlic. Quickly sauté, then add cilantro and black beans.

Incorporate and add Liquid Smoke and brown sugar.
Pour and stir Dijon mustard and ketchup into chili sauce.
Sprinkle chili powder.

Place stock pot on low heat and begin to simmer until most of liquid is absorbed by black beans.

If desired constancy is to have a more pourable bean dish, add few ounces of water to thin.

GREATEST FRIES EVER

With French Fries being the most consumed fast food on the planet, it seems fitting that we throw our signature version in the hat, or at least in the fryer. Fresh-cut and double-fried, they can become very addictive, which means pounds around the waist. You have been warned! Enjoy.

Difficulty: 2

Serves: 4

Prep:

3 Idaho potatoes
2 sweet potatoes
3 parsnips
1 gal peanut oil
kosher sea salt
black pepper

medium stock pot or fryer

In fryer or medium stock pot, heat peanut oil. On cutting board, place rinsed potatoes. Carefully cut Idaho potatoes lengthwise into quarter-inch strips. Repeat steps with all potatoes.

Peel and cut parsnips into quarter-inch sticks. Place potatoes in room-temperature water until oil gets hot. This will help in releasing starches.

Drain potatoes on plate draped with paper towel. When oil is hot, carefully place fries in oil. This will reduce temperature of oil. Cook fries for 5 minutes and carefully remove. Set on cooling plate and place in freezer if you can make room.

When ready to enjoy the fries, reheat peanut oil, remove potatoes from freezer, and place in heated peanut oil. Add parsnips and cook until golden-brown.

Remove and season with salt and pepper.

KOREAN BBQ RIBS

My love for Asian fare is even intensified when talking ribs. The time it takes to make great smoky ribs is enhanced by incorporating Eastern accents, sweet undertones, and contrasting charring on the ribs. These should be eaten in private.

Difficulty: 3

Serves: 4

4 slabs St. Louis ribs
2 Tbsp garlic powder
1 Tbsp ginger spice
2 tsp coriander
1 cup brown sugar
2 tsp red pepper flake
2 tsp black pepper
1 Tbsp kosher sea salt
3 Tbsp sesame seeds
½ cup water
⅓ cup cilantro, chopped

Asian BBQ Sauce (See recipe on page 39.)

large bowl
large baking dish
foil

Note: Grill outdoors.

Prep:

Rinse St Louis ribs with warm water and set on cutting board. Mix all ingredients together in bowl. Start by rubbing mixture on top of all 4 slabs. Use reserved spices for back or underside of ribs. Let ribs stand for at least twenty minutes. Ribs will begin to sweat. This is good.

Preheat outdoor grill and season grate with oil. When grill is hot, place ribs on grill, flesh side down. Cook for five minutes and turn on a 90-degree angle for three minutes. Turn ribs over, on underside, and cook for an additional 5 minutes.

Preheat oven to 350 degrees.
In large baking dish, arrange ribs. Add ½ cup water and chopped cilantro on top of ribs. Cover with foil and cook in oven until tender (about 1 hour and 45 minutes) and remove from oven.

Check tenderness of ribs by bending end of ribs. Ribs should be able to tear away from each other but not shred apart. Remove ribs from oven and baste with Asian BBQ Sauce.

Return to oven, uncovered, and cook for an additional 20 minutes at 300 degrees.

Garnish with sesame seeds and serve.

OVEN ROASTED TURKEY THIGHS WITH MUSHROOM GRAVY

I certainly enjoy turkey and all the trimming for the holidays. There also is a dish that my mother has me hooked on, Oven Roasted Turkey Thighs. Whenever she can grab them from the market, she would call me and invite me over.

Difficulty: 2

Serves: 4

Prep:

2 turkey thighs
1 small onion
4 oz celery (1-inch cut)
4 oz carrots
6 oz mushrooms, sliced
8 oz chicken stock
2 Tbsp thyme
2 Tbsp parsley
1 Tbsp black pepper
2 tsp kosher sea salt
2 oz green onions
2 oz Worcestershire sauce

Roux (See recipe on page 117.)

medium baking dish
medium sauté pan
foil

Preheat oven to 350 degrees.

Rinse turkey thighs and place on cutting board. Score turkey thighs with knife. Coat thighs with ground pepper, thyme, and fresh parsley. Season with salt. Place in lined foiled baking dish. Add chopped onions, celery, and carrots. Pour in 4 oz chicken stock, 2 oz Worcestershire sauce, 2 oz brown sugar, and sage.

Cover with foil and cook for 30 minutes. Uncover and drain liquid into bowl.

In sauté pan, add olive oil. Place into pan mushrooms and green onions. Sauté until mushrooms are tender.

Add to pan Roux and reserved broth from turkey. Stir contents in pan until gravy is formed. Remove celery, onions, and carrots from baking dish. Incorporate vegetables into gravy and bring to simmer.

Cook turkey until fully cooked. Internal temperature should read 165 degrees. Remove from oven when cooked.

Cut turkey from bone and ladle gravy over poultry. Serve with favorite sides.

TOMATO GORGONZOLA DRESSING

Strangely enough, my childhood memories consist of repeated episodes of fresh salads loaded with bleu cheese dressing. Even as a child, I fell in love with the bite and creaminess of bleu cheese. If you're a bleu cheese lover, Point Reyes brand is pricey, but heavenly.

Difficulty: 1

Makes: 2 quarts

Prep:

1 cup gorgonzola cheese
2 oz balsamic vinegar
2 oz tomato paste
1 oz chipotle sauce
1 Tbsp parsley, fresh
1 tsp black pepper
⅓ cup sour cream
½ cup mayo
2 oz parsley, dried
2 oz olive oil

medium mixing bowl
wire whisk

In medium mixing bowl, add bleu cheese, balsamic vinegar, dried parsley, and black pepper. Mix to incorporate.

Add mayo, sour cream, and tomato paste. Fold all ingredients together.

Add 1 tsp chipotle sauce. Drizzle in olive oil and set aside until needed.

If you are like me, I generally add more blue cheese crumbles.

PINEAPPLE TERIYAKI CHICKEN WINGS

One of my NFL Pro Bowl clients would have me make this sauce and smother St. Louis baby back ribs. I also love this tasty delight on chicken wings. It makes a great finger food.

Difficulty: 1

Serves: 4

Prep:

3 lbs chicken wing pieces
⅓ cup soy sauce
2 tsp garlic, minced
2 tsp ginger, minced
1 cup pineapple juice
⅓ cup brown sugar
½ tsp red pepper flake
1 Tbsp parsley
3 oz onion, minced
1 tsp hot chili sauce, Sriracha
2 tsp lemon pepper
1 oz extra virgin olive oil

medium sauce pan
lined baking dish

Note: Grill outdoors.

Rinse and rub chicken pieces to ensure they are free of debris, feathers, etc.
Season with lemon pepper.

Preheat grill for cooking. When hot, season grates and toss wing pieces on grill. Cook on all sides for 10 minutes. This is to sear and char lemon pepper on chicken.

Remove from grill and place in bowl while you make sauce.

In medium sauce pan, add olive oil. Add minced onion, garlic, and ginger. Add pineapple juice and chili sauce. Add brown sugar and soy sauce and let reduce until thick.

Toss grilled chicken pieces in teriyaki sauce. Remove and spread on lined baking dish. Cook in preheated oven 350 degrees for twenty minutes. Uncover the last five minutes.

GREEK SALAD WITH
GRILLED LEMON PEPPER SHRIMP

What salad is more flavorful than an perfectly dressed Greek Salad? I do not know of many. We top this one off with tasty lemon pepper shrimp.

Difficulty: 1

Serves: 4

12 tiger shrimp (U-15)
4 oz kalamata olives, pitted
1 tomato (diced)
4 oz cucumbers, diced
3 oz red onion, sliced
8 oz feta cheese
12 oz romaine lettuce (1-inch cut)
6 oz spinach (cut or tear large leaves)
8 oz baby mixed green lettuce
3 oz lemon pepper

3 oz red wine vinegar
3 oz extra virgin olive oil
1 tsp garlic, chopped
1 tsp sugar
1 tsp fresh thyme
1 tsp oregano
½ tsp black pepper

grill plate or outdoor grill
medium mixing bowl
wire whisk

Prep:

In medium mixing bowl, place all rinsed clean lettuces, romaine, spinach, and baby greens. Incorporate together and set aside until needed.

In small bowl, mix red wine vinegar, garlic, sugar, and herbs. Slowly whisk in extra virgin olive oil. Set dressing aside until needed.

On salad plate or bowl, arrange a small mound of mixed salad greens. Add cucumbers, olives, and sliced red onion.
Garnish with 2 oz feta cheese crumbles and set in refrigerator until needed.

Preparing Shrimp:
Place peeled and deveined shrimp in bowl.
Lightly sprinkle with lemon pepper.
Let stand for 10 minutes.

Preheat grill for cooking. When grill is hot, season with oil. Place shrimp on grill and cook through, turning shrimp on each side, but be careful not to over-char.

Remove salad from refrigerator and set before guests. Top with Grilled Lemon Pepper Shrimp and enjoy.

CARAMELIZED DUCK BREAST

Duck, one of my sinful culinary treats, is so rich with flavor and such a versatile poultry. I enjoy scoring the fat side of the duck and rendering crisp before finishing in oven. The contrast in the meat texture and the crisp skin is sheer delight with every mouthful.

Difficulty: 2

Serves: 6

Prep:

6 duck breasts (boneless)
½ cup green onions
¼ cup fresh ginger
1 fresh oranges
1 cup orange Juice
4 garlic cloves
⅓ cup fresh cilantro
1 tsp black pepper
1 tsp kosher sea salt
2 tsp olive oil
1 tsp chopped ginger
4 oz chicken stock

medium sauté pan
small baking dish

Ginger Orange Juice Marinade:
Place in baking dish, one cup orange juice, crushed garlic, cilantro, 1 tsp chopped ginger.
Add 2 tsp olive oil.
Add 1 tsp black pepper.
Mix together an reserve until duck is prepared and trimmed.

Duck Breast:
Rinse duck breast and place on cutting board. Separate breast lobes, if needed.
On fat cap of duck, make incisions, creating an X, twice on duck breast.
Place duck breast in marinade and cover for 1 hour in chilled area.

In medium skillet, heat olive oil.
When oil is heated, remove duck breast from marinade.
Sprinkle with flour and shake excess.
Place skin side down in skillet and cook, turning until golden-brown.
Turn down heat on skillet. Turn duck breast and quickly sear other side for 1 minute. Remove from pan and place in small baking dish.
Squeeze oranges into bowl, then add ginger and 4 oz chicken stock to freshly squeezed orange juice.
Add fresh chopped cilantro.
Remove duck breast when internal temperature reaches 165 degrees.
Slice on cutting board and arrange on plate. Pour orange ginger juice over duck and enjoy.

ROASTED PEAR AND SPINACH SALAD

Delicious Bosc pears add an unexpected sweetness to this healthy spinach salad.

Difficulty: 1

Serves: 2

8 oz spinach
2 Bosc pears
4 oz dried cranberries
½ red onions
2 oz olive oil
1 tsp cracked black pepper
4 oz goat cheese
4 oz shitake mushrooms
vegetable oil

Dressing:
½ cup balsamic vinegar
⅓ cup extra virgin olive oil
2 oz agave (raw)
1 Tbsp dried parsley
½ tsp pepper flake

small sauté pan
small and medium bowls

Prep:

Preheat oven to 325 degrees.

Rinse Bosc pears and place on cutting board. Cut in half and carefully cut out any seeds. Place on baking sheet and drizzle a little olive oil on them. Season with salt and pepper. Roast in preheated oven for 12 minutes. Remove from oven and set aside until needed.

Dressing:
In small bowl, add all ingredients except olive oil. Mix ingredients and slowly drizzle in olive oil. Continue to mix until fully incorporated. Set aside until needed.

Crispy Shitake Mushrooms:
In small sauté pan, add vegetable oil and heat until hot. Place sliced mushrooms in hot oil. Fry until golden-brown and they begin to shrivel up a bit. Drain on paper towel and lightly dust with salt.

In medium bowl, place chopped spinach, sliced red onions, chilled roasted pears, and dried cranberries. Pour in dressing, being careful not to over-dress the salad. Arrange in separate salad bowls. Top with crispy shitake mushrooms and garnish with cubed goat cheese.

MEATBALL PERFECTO

These meatballs have been challenged by the most discriminating palates. They have stood the test of time, and I am delighted to share them with you. Ladies, if you just happen to add them to some timeless spaghetti noodles, I am not responsible for what happens at your dinner table.

Difficulty: 1

Serves: 4

Prep:

12 oz ground beef (80/20)
8 oz ground veal
4 oz ground pork
1 onion, small-diced
2 oz thyme
2 Tbsp garlic
4 oz diced tomato
8 oz tomato sauce
4 oz parmesan cheese
1 Tbsp dried basil

medium baking dish
large bowl

In medium sauté pan, add olive oil, garlic, and onion. Sauté until garlic browns a bit and onion has saturated the garlic flavors. They will still have some bite left in them. You need the contrast texture in these delicate meat balls.

In a large bowl, mix ground meats. Knead together with your hands to evenly distribute all types throughout meat balls. Place sautéed garlic and onion in mixture. Also add ground basil, fresh thyme, and parmesan cheese. Mix these ingredients together and incorporate until it forms one large ball.
Slowly pour in tomatoes puree. Combine puree into meatball mixture and let stand for 5 minutes, covered.

Take a small ice cream scoop and begin to scoop ground meat. Place on baking dish or plate. When they have all been scooped, gently form the meatballs with your hands, not patting them too tightly.

In preheated oven at 350 degrees place meatballs in baking dish. Cover with shallow layer of tomato sauce. Cook until meatballs are deep brown and cooked through (internal temperature should be 155 degrees). Roll meatballs in sauce in baking dish.

Ladies, feel free to add your favorite pasta or use these amazing meatballs as a standalone dish.

THAI VEGETABLE SOUP WITH
TEMPURA VEGETABLES

Great soup is one of my gauges with many of my chef colleagues. I enjoy the delightful warming elixirs and I seen to try soup everywhere I dine. I tried an amazing Thai soup and was hooked on its simplicity but extreme depth. I think you will enjoy it.

Difficulty: 2

Serves: 4

3 oz scallions, chopped
3 oz lemon grass, peeled and chopped
1 Tbsp ginger, minced
2 oz sesame oil
2 oz fresh lime juice
½ tsp red pepper flake
4 cups vegetable stock
2 oz fresh cilantro
2 oz dried parsley
3 oz carrots (thin sticks)
4 oz celery, peeled
8 slices onion (tempura)
6 shitake (sliced, tempura)
6 red Holland peppers

Tempura;
12 oz olive oil
⅓ cup water
¼ cup flour
2 Tbsp sugar
½ cup cornstarch

medium stock pot
small sauce pan

Prep:

Preheat stovetop.

Heat medium stock pot and add sesame oil. Quickly add ginger, lemon grass, scallions, and then sauté. Add cilantro and pour in vegetable stock. Add fresh lime juice and allow to simmer.

While broth is simmering, heat 12 ounces of olive oil in small sauce pan. In separate bowl, add egg, flour, sugar, dried parsley, and lime zest.
Mix all to smooth consistency.

On cutting board, slice each red Holland pepper into 6 rings. (Each ring should be about ½-inch thick.)

In separate bowl, place cornstarch and salt.
Place vegetables in bowl of cornstarch.
Remove excess cornstarch and dip vegetables in egg mixtures.
Hold over heated oil and place halfway in until it starts to cook. Then let vegetables sink in heated grease. The vegetables will float quickly. Cook for 30 seconds and remove. Drain on plate. Reserve until needed.

Taste broth. Salt to taste or add one teaspoon of soy sauce. Place celery and carrots in bottom of bowl. Ladle soup over vegetables. Before serving, arrange tempura vegetables and serve with large spoon.

SPICED CLAM CHOWDER

Growing up in the Tri-State area, sharing time in Philadelphia and New Jersey, I developed a love for seafood and an obsession for Italian sausage. This recipe was developed to cure two culinary desires at once. It works well with the spicy Italian sausage, or without Italian sausage for a classic creamy clam chowder.

Difficulty: 3

Serves: 6

Prep:

12 fresh clams
10 oz clams, chopped
⅓ cup onion diced
½ cup celery diced
3 strips bacon, cut into small strips
½ cup sausage, Italian rope, spicy
1 cup Yukon Gold potato, diced
4 cups clam stock
¾ cup heavy cream
2 Bay Leaves
1½ Tbsp Old Bay Seasoning
kosher sea salt
black pepper
1 bunch parsley (Italian)
2 tsp garlic, chopped
¼ cup thyme fresh

Roux (See recipe on page 117.)

medium stock pot

Use a medium stock pot to first make clam stock, and reserve liquid after you strain debris, if any.

Clam Stock:
Place rinsed whole clams in bottom of stock pot. Tip: Stand the clams on their backs so they will open quicker. Cover the clams with water ,halfway covering clams.
Add 1 tsp salt and fresh parsley. Turn on heat and bring to boil. The clams should begin to open. When they are open, allow to simmer for 5 minutes. Remove clams and set aside until needed.
Place 1 tsp chopped garlic in liquid, and add 3 cups of water. Placed diced potato in clam stock and cook until almost tender. Remove them from stock and reserve.
Carefully strain clam stock into separate bowl, removing any debris that may have settled on the bottom.
In the same medium stock pot, add olive oil, onions, celery, and bacon. Cook until bacon is almost cooked, then add chopped Italian sausage, and cook through.
Place chopped clams in stock pot. Place in bay leaf, Old Bay Seasoning, and clam stock.
Add fresh thyme.
Allow to simmer for 10 minutes. Pour cream into stock pot and bring to simmer. Add Roux to thicken to desired consistency.
Place diced potato and whole clams into stock pot. Season with kosher sea salt and black pepper to taste.

HONEY GLAZED GAME HEN

Whenever I get the chance to have guests over, I try to change their opinions about eating chicken vs. game hens. I adore the sweeter tasting smaller birds, although this recipe also lends well to chicken or duck. You decide.

Difficulty: 2

Serves: 4

2 game hens (about 2½ lbs each)
1 large sweet onion
1 carrot
2 celery stalks
1 small jar of honey
1 tsp ground pepper
1 tsp kosher sea salt
½ tsp garlic pepper
1 tsp chili powder

medium roasting pan
foil

Prep:

Ensure the game hens are thawed completely. Remove any items from the bird membrane. Rinse in cool water and set aside. Line baking dish with foil for easy cleaning.

Preheat oven to 350 degrees.

Clean and chop carrot, celery, and onion into one-inch pieces. Evenly distribute in roasting pan. Rub game hens with garlic pepper and chili powder. Place in roasting pan. Add one teaspoon of honey to the inside of each bird.

Mix 4 oz honey, 1 tsp ground pepper, and 1 tsp salt in cup and set aside.

Cook in oven for 15 minutes.
Remove from oven and glaze with honey mixture.
Cook for additional 15 minutes. Internal temperature should reach 165 degrees.

PHILADELPHIA FILET STEAK SANDWICH

This cookbook would not be complete without my favorite hometown sandwich. The Philadelphia Steak Sandwich is world-renown. There are many places in Philly to go, but I have to say that Gennaro's (now on Bainbridge Street, was on South Street) is my all-time favorite.

Difficulty : 1

Serves: 2

Prep:

1 lb beef filet
1 small onion white, sliced
½ cup green peppers
2 hoagie rolls
6 slices smoked provolone cheese
2 Tbsp mayo (optional)
1 tsp kosher salt
1 tsp ground pepper
ketchup (optional)

medium sauté pan
3 oz olive oil

Place filet medallions on cutting board and pound thin. Set aside until needed
Slice onions thin and set aside.
Slice green peppers and set aside.

Place medium sauté pan on stove top.
Place on medium-high heat.
Add olive oil
Place onions and peppers in olive oil, cooking quickly.
Place in pounded filet meat and sprinkle with kosher salt and pepper.

Quickly incorporate all items.
Cook steak fully.
Place sliced provolone cheese on top.
Spread mayo on hoagie roll, if desired.
Place roll on top of cheese.
Remove from heat and let stand for 3 minutes.

Place spatula under meat and onions and peppers.
Remove steak sandwich from sauté pan.
Place on plate and cut in half.
Add desired sauces and serve hot.

ANGUS BEEF STEW EN CROUTE

Nothing warms the inside like a hearty beef stew. With the addition of flaky puff pastry, this ageless classic gets an overhaul of texture and flavors. If you can find small baking dishes, you can make ahead of time or even freeze them.

Difficulty: 2

Serves: 6

Prep:

1½ lbs angus beef, cubed
1 cup Yukon Gold potato, diced small
½ cup red onions, diced
½ cup carrots, diced
¼ cup celery, diced
2 cups beef stock
½ cup peas
¼ cup parsley, chopped
1 Tbsp oregano, chopped
1 cup red wine
2 Tbsp Roux (See recipe on page 117.)
3 frozen puff pastry sheets
¼ cup butter, melted
1 egg
¼ cup water
1 Tbsp garlic salt
2 Tbsp brown sugar

small baking dishes

Place medium stock pot on stove top. Place on medium heat.

Add olive oil. Season beef cubes with garlic salt, parsley, and brown sugar.

Quickly sauté and add potatoes, celery, and onions. Add red wine, and beef stock.
Add oregano.
Cook on low heat until potatoes are tender.
Add Roux when potatoes are cooked tender.
Add soy sauce and Worcestershire sauce.
Set aside while you prepare baking dishes.

Preheat oven to 350 degrees.
Place baking dishes on baking sheet so you can easily remove from oven when cooked.
Make egg wash by placing one egg in bowl with water. Whisk until incorporated.
Thaw puff pastry and cut into squares large enough to cover top of baking dishes.

Fill baking dishes with savory beef stew. Cover with puff pastry, sealing over baking dishes by pinching closed with fingers.
Poke small holes in crust with fork. Brush top of pastry with egg wash.
Bake in preheated oven until bubbly hot and pastry is golden-brown.

BRAISED OX TAILS

By far, my favorite everyday meal. I was introduced to island fare from a friend of my youth, and have been hooked ever since.

Difficulty: 2

Serves: 4

5 lbs ox tails
1 large white onion
1 cup celery
1 cup carrots
1 Tbsp chopped garlic
2 Tbsp cumin
¼ cup parsley
2 Tbsp ground black pepper
1½ cup red wine
2 cup chicken stock
2 Tbsp Worcestershire sauce
2 Tbsp soy sauce
2 Tbsp brown sugar
1 cup diced tomatoes, in juice
2 oz cornstarch
2 cups short-grain rice
2 bay leaves
½ cup pico mixture (minced celery, onion, and peppers)
2 cups vegetable stock
¼ cup cilantro
1 cup water

Seasoned flour:
1 cup flour
2 tsp kosher salt
1 tsp ground black pepper
1 tsp garlic

Prep:

Rinse ox tails and set aside on large plate.
Season with dry spices, coating both sides.
Place ox tail in bag of seasoned flour and shake until evenly coated.
Heat oil in a large sauté pan or braising pot. When oil is heated, carefully place ox tails in sauté pan. Cook on both sides until golden-brown, reducing heat so you do not burn drippings. (They will be used for an amazing rich sauce.)
Preheat oven to 350 degrees. Remove ox tails from sauté pan and place in roasting or baking pan. Top with fresh parsley. Add chicken stock, Worcestershire sauce, and soy sauce. Pour in one cup of water, add bay leaf, and cover with foil.
Bake in preheated oven for 90 minutes. Carefully open foil, add chopped celery, onion, and carrots to roasting pan. Add tomatoes (with juice) to pan and reseal foil over ox tails. Cook until fork-tender, about another 45 minutes to one hour. When tender, remove from pan and reserve the stock for sauce.

Assembly:

In medium sauce pan, add 2 cups rice, add bay leaf, 1 cup vegetable stock, and 1 cup of water.
Place a tsp of roasted chopped garlic. Place heat on low and cover until liquid is halfway removed. Stir in pico mixture (celery, onions, and peppers). Cook until liquid is removed and rice is tender. Salt and pepper to taste.
Set aside until needed.

Red Wine Sauce:
In small sauce pan, add oil, chopped garlic, and celery. Cook on medium heat. When garlic is slightly brown, add red wine. Stir in brown sugar and chopped cilantro, and then reduce by half.
Add 1½ cups of beef stock (produced from ox tails) to sauce. Let simmer for 5 minutes. Place cornstarch in 2 oz water and pour into sauce. Let reduce until desired constancy.
Heat all items and place ox tails on top of heated rice. Ladle sauce over ox tails and rice.

CRISPY CALAMARI LEMON PEPPER

Lemon pepper is a wonderful way to seduce calamari lovers. When cooking these amazing rings, we blend the pepper with cornmeal and flour. Pair with red sauce or an citrus aioli.

Difficulty: 2

Serves: 4

Prep:

1½ lbs calamari rings and tentacles
1 cup flour
⅓ cup cornmeal
2 Tbsp lemon pepper
1 tsp red pepper flake
1 tsp kosher salt
2 eggs
¼ cup water
1 Tbsp lemon juice
vegetable juice

medium stock pot
strainer basket
drip plate

Rinse calamari pieces in cool water and allow to drain.
In separate bowl, mix flour, cornmeal, lemon pepper, and red pepper flake. Set aside until ready to fry.

In small bowl, mix eggs, water, and lemon juice.
Mix until smooth, then add calamari pieces.

Place medium stock pot on stove top.
Add vegetable oil and place on high heat.
When oil is ready (determined by fry test), remove a few calamari pieces from lemon egg wash, place in flour mixture, fully coating the calamari pieces.
Remove excess flour.
Carefully place in heated oil and cook until golden.
Repeat process with remaining calamari pieces.
Set on draining dish and remove pot from heated surface when finished.

Serve with favorite dipping sauce.
Enjoy!

A Way To A Woman's Heart
Questionnaire

1. *When, how, and why do you give your heart to your partner?*
2. *What scares you about love or falling in love?*
3. *When are you secure in a relationship?*
4. *What made your first love special?*
5. *What do partners need to understand about a woman's heart?*
6. *How should a partner approach a woman?*
7. *Do partners try too hard?*
8. *When has a partner challenged the trust in a relationship?*
9. *How should a partner communicate their love to a woman?*
10. *How important is your partner's physical attributes?*
11. *How important is your partner's educational background?*
12. *How important is your partner's relationships with other woman?*
13. *How important is your partner's relationship with God?*
14. *How important is your partner's relationships with his family?*
15. *How important is your partner's relationships with friends?*
16. *What specific types of conversation keep you interested?*
17. *What makes you laugh in a relationship?*
18. *What makes you cry in a relationship?*
19. *What makes you try harder to please your partner?*
20. *What makes you give up in a relationship?*
21. *How can your partner make you feel beautiful?*
22. *How can your partner make you feel not so beautiful?*
23. *What are important compliments to conquer your heart?*
24. *How important is it for you to receive little gifts from your partner?*
25. *How important is time spent together with your partner?*
26. *What personal values must a partner have to conquer your heart?*
27. *What ethical values must a partner have to conquer your heart?*
28. *What religious values must a partner have to conquer your heart?*
29. *What work values must a partner have to conquer your heart?*
30. *What business values must a partner have to conquer your heart?*
31. *Why should a partner invest time getting to know their woman?*
32. *What should a partner do get to know their woman?*
33. *How can a partner restore your trust in a relationship?*
34. *How can your partner mend your broken heart?*
35. *Do partners usually know what women like or dislike, sexually?*
36. *How do you let your partner know your intimate desires?*
37. *Do partners tell their woman they love them enough—everyday?*
38. *Do partners take enough time to make passionate love to their woman?*
39. *Do partners communicate their sexual desires to their woman?*
40. *Do partners accommodate their woman's physical needs and desires?*

41. *Do partners accommodate their woman's emotional needs and desires?*

42. *Do partners accommodate their woman's sexual needs and desires?*

43. *Does your partner take you out on dates regularly?*

44. *Does your partner add to your happiness and life's pleasures?*

45. *Does your partner drain your happiness and life's pleasures?*

46. *Do partners really know what women want and need?*

47. *Do partners often play games or lie at the onset of relationships?*

48. *Do partners lie to keep you in a dead-end and unproductive relationship?*

49. *Do partners lie to keep you in a violent or unhealthy relationship?*

50. *Do partners tell woman what they are looking for in a relationship?*

51. *Are partners honest about what they want and don't want from a relationship?*

52. *How can partners always let women know they love them?*

53. *How can partners show they love who you are—inside and outside?*

54. *How important is it for your partner to share in cooking and cleaning the house?*

55. *Do partners try to be too masculine and insensitive in love relationships?*

56. *What do you desire most in a partner?*

57. *What do you desire least in a partner?*

58. *Do you find partners or dates will say anything to get what they want?*

59. *What to you despise most in a relationship?*

60. *What do you love most in a relationship?*

61. *Do partners make an effort to know and get along with your family?*

62. *Do partners make an effort to know and get along with your friends?*

63. *Are you turned-on or turned-off when hit-on during the first date? Why?*

64. *Do you think it's okay to have sex on the first date? Why?*

65. *Do you think it's okay to make love on the first date? Why?*

66. *Do you let your partner know all your needs as a woman? Why?*

67. *Do you feel comfortable communicating all your intimate needs?*

68. *Does your partner have to be a High School graduate? Why?*

69. *Does your partner have to be a college graduate? Why?*

70. *Does your partner have to have their own a car? Why?*

71. *Does your partner have to have their own place to live? Why?*

72. *Does your partner have to have steady employment? Why?*

73. *Does your partner have to have a good-paying job? Why?*

74. *Does your partner have to be married? Why?*

75. *Does your partner have to be single? Why?*

76. *How does a woman know if her partner loves her?*

77. *How does a woman know if her partner is in love with her?*

78. *What is the difference between "love" and "in love" in a relationship?*

79. *What makes a woman fall in love with her partner?*

80. *What makes a woman fall out of love with her partner?*

81. *How important is your partner's vision and goals for the future?*

82. *What usually are women's goals in a relationship?*

83. *What usually are your partner's goals in a relationship?*

84. *Do you often find yourself in self-defeating relationships?*

85. *Do women often settle for partners for reasons other than love?*

86. *What reasons cause women to settle for Mr. Wrong?*

87. *Do partners often settle for women for reasons other than love?*

88. *What reasons cause partners to settle for Ms./Mrs. Wrong?*

89. *Do you believe that love is enough to sustain a relationship? Why?*

90. *How important to you is pleasing your partner in every way?*

91. *How important is your partner pleasing you in every way?*

92. *Do partners know women's basic needs: food, shelter, love, security, etc.?*

93. *Do partners know your clothes size, eye color, favorite color, movie, food, etc.?*

94. *How can your partner make you feel more secure in your relationship?*

95. *What do you do to let your partner know you want to make love—right now?*

96. *How should partners approach their women when they want to make love?*

97. *How should partners approach their women when they want to have wild sex?*

98. *Where is the most romantic or exciting place your partner has ever taken you?*

99. *What is the most exciting thing that your partner has ever done for you?*

100. *How can your partner make you forget you are angry or frustrated?*

101. *Do you prefer a partner you can predict or not predict? Why?*

102. *Do you believe that best friends make great lovers? Why?*

103. *Do you believe that best friends make great partners? Why?*

104. *Where are some great places to make love?*

105. *What's the best time of the day to make love? Why?*

106. *Is make-up sex really great and all it is claimed to be? Why?*

107. *How can your partner blow your mind in bed?*

108. *How can your partner blow your mind physically and emotionally?*

109. *Does your partner share your feelings in triumphs, trials, and tribulations?*

110. *Does your partner make you feel safe and secure? How?*

111. *Does your partner make you feel proud? How?*

112. *Does your partner make you feel alive vs. just existing day-to-day? How?*

113. *Does your partner make you feel jealous of other friends and family? How?*

114. *Does your partner make you feel that you can conquer the world? How?*

How does your relationship measure up?

NOTES

NOTES

NOTES

NOTES

NOTES

ABOUT THE AUTHOR

Celebrity Chef Michael Stevenson is a self-made entrepreneur, a United States Navy veteran, founder and CEO of Experience Hospitality, LLC, and an author. His first book—**The Greatest Ingredient in the World: Forgiveness**—is a soul-serving novel. This, his second book—**A Way To A Woman's Heart: The Cookbook**—is a unique and romantic cookbook that provides a clever comparison between food, love, passion, intimacy, and relationships.

Food Visionary and Service Aficionado are words that clearly define Chef Michael Stevenson. His food is creative, bold, and expressive, yet refined to satisfy the most discriminating of guests. Chef Mike's approach to food is a perpetual art form. From his early teens, he has entrancingly evolved from concocting a new and improved pancake mix from scratch to running some of the most powerful dinning houses across America.

With his signature line of cooking spices, every kitchen is a platform to perform his "food art" and succulent masterpieces. Not knowing if the cameras are off or on, Chef Mike is a sheer delight to watch in and out of the kitchen. He began honing his cooking palate in landmark restaurants on the New Jersey shore, such as Longport Inn, and in the Philadelphia area, such as Moshulu, Paradigm, and Ritz Carlton, before entering the United Sates Navy. Then, Operations Specialist Air Traffic Controller Michael Stevenson served his country in the first installment of troops to Kuwait. During his tour, Chef Mike traveled the world, expanding his commitment to food, faith, and family, and shaping his future as a celebrated chef, author, and entrepreneur.

Born and raised in South Philadelphia, he has developed the innate Rocky spirit. Chef Mike's passion and pursuit of culinary excellence drove him to commit to working and mastering every facet of the restaurant and hospitality industry. Always re-inventing himself, Chef Mike has spent countless hours in the kitchen perfecting his culinary craft. Committed to his personal goal to train only under the best chefs in his field, he set out on a tour of apprenticeship/mentorship from Five-Diamond hotels and Italian eateries to high-volume steak-and-chop houses, such as the famed Le Cirque 2000 in Manhattan.

Determined to refine his food artistry and craft, Chef Mike aggressively sought to enhance his pastry knowledge and perfect his skills under world-famous Pastry Chef Jacque Torres at Le Cirque 2000 at the Palace Hotel in New York. Always the quick study, he pursued and engulfed himself into the world of various celebrated chefs. He has taken his "lessons learned" and his innate gifts from the confines of their elaborate restaurant kitchens to the homes of Hollywood celebrities, illustrious entertainers, renowned political figures, and NFL team owners and players.

Author, Entrepreneur, and Celebrity Chef Michael Stevenson is the founder of **Experience Hospitality, LLC**, an event management company which provides five-star culinary service and exquisite lifestyle products and services to elite clients with discriminating taste and style. Specializing in delectable cuisines, Chef Mike prepares award-winning fare with the freshest produce and savory ingredients.

The **Chef Mike Experience** was birthed one plate and meal at a time. Following the success of Chef Michael Stevenson's creative provisions, the demand for his exclusive services included special after-hour meals for entertainers, who hired him as a personal chef for their homes and private events. Whether providing a romantic dinner for two or an elaborate soiree, **Experience Hospitality, LLC** is committed to excellent services, first-rate catering, and unique products that elevate any event to a lifestyle of elegance and great taste.

To ensure a momentous and eventful affair, **Experience Hospitality, LLC** implements **three core elements**:

1. **Cutting-edge Menu Design** — Our foods and spirits lure and satisfy your guests' discerning tastes as well as the procurement of fine and organic foods upon request.
2. **World Class Service** — We partner with the industry's top service aficionados and offer amenities that surpass our clients' expectations.
3. **Exquisite Logistics and Staging** — Each client is granted a one-on-one consultation before event planning. We issue timely contracts and provide 24-hour call center service for any last-minute requests.

Experience Hospitality, LLC's outstanding services and products include, but are not limited to:

Weddings
Reunions
Anniversaries
College Events
Social Events
Public Relations Events
Political Events
Charity and Humanitarian Events
Seminars
Cooking Classes and Demonstrations
Speaking Engagements
Radio and TV Appearances
Hospitality Food and Business Consultation
Lifestyle and Travel Consultation
New Line of Spices
Health and Fitness Meal Programs
Book (novel): The Greatest Ingredient In The World: Forgiveness
Cookbook: A Way To A Woman's Heart

WANTED

Women Seeking a Great Job Opportunity and Experience
Become a Chef Mike Partner and Earn Income $$$$$ for 2013.
Chef Mike is looking for partners to share in the success of his new cookbook:
A Way To A Woman's Heart

Experience Hospitality, LLC is offering Chef Mike partnerships and employment opportunities to ladies interested in hosting romance-themed parties to introduce the new cookbook—**A Way To A Woman's Heart**—to your invited guests. Your income, sales incentives, and partnership gifts will be based on the number of books sold and new Chef Mike partnerships initiated at your party/book event.

Chef Mike has created this concept to provide all women across America an amazing opportunity to earn extra income during the recession, share in making 2013 the "year of romance", and help women and their partners of all walks of life and around the world come together as one cohesive family and partnership.

If you enroll and commit, you will be provided all the necessary materials, details, and resources to prepare you to become a successful party host and *Chef Mike Partner*. Exciting sales incentives and gifts will be awarded to all motivated campaign partners who produce results in book sales and new partnerships!

If you become a partner, you must be willing to promote **A Way To A Woman's Heart** by hosting a party or event that meets company guidelines, invite your friends, coworkers, family members, or potential customers and partners and introduce them to the **Chef Mike Experience**, the new cookbook, and other products and services. During the romance-themed parties and events, your guests will get an up-close and personal look at Chef Mike (by viewing a video produced by Chef Mike), his sensual cookbook, **A Way To A Woman's Heart**, his soul-serving novel, **The Greatest Ingredient in the World: Forgiveness**, and other products and services.

Your hosted event will be a great opportunity for invited guests to become partners (earn income), buy Chef Mike's books, and place orders for other products and services, to include event appearances, catering, seminars, cooking classes and demonstrations. In exchange for opening up your home as a *Chef Mike Partner*, you will receive merchandise gifts, sales incentives, and income proportional in value to the amount of books sold and new partnerships initiated. **We look forward to working with you in 2013, the "year of romance".**

To apply, contact Chef Mike by email (mike@chefmike.tv) or by phone at 757-338-3274.

Experience Hospitality, LLC

Chef Mike Stevenson & Dr. Jessie Gee

BOOK ORDER FORM

Please print all requested information. You may call 210-846-8599 or email your orders.

A Way To A Woman's Heart: The Cookbook _____ @ 27.97 = _____ Total

The Greatest Ingredient In The World: Forgiveness _____ @ 12.95 = _____ Total

Name: _____

Address: _____

_____

City: _____ State _____ Zip _____

Phone: _____Cell_____

Email (Optional): _____

Note: Providing your email and phone number will help us to expedite your order if we need clarification on any items.

Credit Card Orders:

-
Type of Card: (MasterCard, Visa, Discover, etc.) _____

Card#: _____

Expiration Date: _____

Signature of Cardholder: _____

Sub Total: $_____

Tax: $_____

Shipping: $4.95* (One book per transaction)

*For shipping fees on orders of more than one book, call us at 210-846-6599 or email us at sales@chefmike.tv.

Total $_____

Money Order Enclosed: _____

PayPal Payment: _____

Sorry, we do not accept personal checks for <u>any</u> book orders, products or services.

Thank You.

THE GREATEST INGREDIENT IN THE WORLD

Forgiveness

A Soul Serving Novel

BY MICHAEL STEVENSON

GLOSSARY OF COOKING TERMS

Here's a quick reference for some of the cooking terms:

GENERAL TERMS

Brine, Brining: To infuse flavor through submersion of protein in liquid.

Char (shrimp): Quickly searing spices on skin of shrimp.

Deglaze: To extract flavor from pan by adding wine or liquid.

Fold: Mixing without removing air, gently. Usually with a spatula.

Fragrant: Aroma from cooking, when heat is added to cooking.

Frigid: Cold, cold to touch or colder water.

Fry-Ready Test: Test done before frying items. Place a drop of flour in heated oil, and if it starts to sizzle, the oil is hot and ready for frying.

Incorporate: To mix ingredient together, one to another.

Ladle: Utensil used for pouring liquids from containers.

Mince: Smaller than a normal dice.

Pulse: A gauge on a mixer. A small burst of mixing.

Render, rendering (bacon): Extraction of fat or juices.

Score (turkey thighs): Cut into thick skin to allow easier flavor penetration.

Sear, Searing: Cooking on high heat to cook seasoning on to meats.

Translucent: Light in color almost clear, an onion can turn when cooked

FOOD ITEMS

Roux: butter and flour mixture to aid in thickening sauces, soups, etc.

INDEX

Appetizers, Snacks, & Hors d'oeuvres
Beer Batter Onion Rings, 120
Candied Mixed Nuts, 25
Curry Tiger Shrimp Satays, 89
Fig and Fennel Stuffed Baked Brie, 29
Garlic Mashed Cauliflower, 42
Greatest Fries Ever, 135
Lamb Pineapple Teriyaki Chicken Wings, 139
Lamb Sliders with Cranberry Mayo, 119
Portabella Fries, 18
Roasted Pepper Hummus, 24
Shrimp Cocktail, 23
Tapenade, 26
Wild Mushroom Ragout, 43
BBQ
BBQ Black Beans, 134
Bourbon BBQ Game Hens, 88
Korean BBQ Ribs, 136
Beef
Angus Beef Stew En Croute, 148
Billion Dollar Chili, 51
Braised Beef Short Ribs, 66
Calf Liver Smothered in Sweet Onion Gravy, 121
Ground Bison Meatloaf with Cremini Mushroom Gravy, 122
Meatball Perfecto, 143
Philadelphia Filet Steak Sandwich, 147
Desserts
Granny Smith Apple Bread Pudding, 81
Dressings, Gravies, Marinades, & Sauces
Asian BBQ Sauce, 39
Caesar Dressing, 19
Dijon Tarragon Herb Mayo, 20
Dried Cranberry Mayo, 30
Fig and Fennel Relish, 28
Fresh Herb Brine, 69
Fresh Tomato Marinara, 100
Root Beer BBQ Sauce, 50
Roux (Quick Version), 117
Spicy Sausage Dressing, 52
Tempura Mandarin Chili Sauce, 61
Tomato Gorgonzola Dressing, 138
Grain
Golden Raisin and Scallion Quinoa, 126
Wild Rice Stuffed Salmon, 92
Gumbo
Stadium Gumbo, 41
Meats
Blackened New Zealand Lamb Chops, 82

Braised Ox Tails, 149
Grass-Fed Veal Parm with Puree Eggplant, 83
Ground Bison Meatloaf with Cremini Mushroom Gravy, 122
Lamb Sliders with Cranberry Mayo, 119
Meatball Perfecto, 143

Pasta
Asian Vegetable Soba Noodles, 107
Crawfish Mac and Cheese, 101
Jersey Shore Clams and Linguine, 105
Mozzarella Ravioli with Spicy Sausage, 102
Saffron Mussels, 103
Spicy Ground Turkey Sausage Lasagna, 106
Spinach Fettuccine Alfredo, 104
Spinach Ricotta Cheese Gnocchi with Garlic Cream Sauce, 125

Pork
Korean BBQ Ribs, 136
Mozzarella Ravioli with Spicy Sausage, 102
Smothered Bone-on Pork Chops, 116

Potatoes
Citrus Poached Yams, 46
Greatest Fries Ever, 135
Mashed Basil Sweet Potatoes, 60
Potato Chip Crusted Crab Cakes, 65

POULTRY
Bourbon BBQ Game Hens, 88
Cajun Fried Turkey, 68
Caramelized Duck Breast, 141
Honey Glazed Game Hen, 146
Oven Roasted Turkey Thighs with Mushroom Gravy, 137
Pineapple Teriyaki Chicken Wings, 139
Roasted Turkey Panini, 31
Spicy Ground Turkey Sausage Lasagna, 106

Salads
Bibb Bleu Cheese and Bacon Salad, 90
Chilled Crab Pasta Salad, 74
Chopped Salad, 27
Ciabatta Croutons, 32
Golden Beet, Cucumber, and Tomato Salad, 85
Greek Salad with Grilled Lemon Pepper Shrimp, 140
Heirloom Tomato Caprese, 22
Roasted Pear and Spinach Salad, 142

Seafood
Chilean Sea Bass in Smoked Tomato Sauce, 124
Chilled Crab Pasta Salad, 74
Crawfish Étouffée, 118
Crawfish Mac and Cheese, 101
Crispy Calamari Lemon Pepper, 150
Crispy Salmon Cakes, 86
Curry Tiger Shrimp Satays, 89
Greek Salad with Grilled Lemon Pepper Shrimp, 140

Jersey Shore Clams and Linguine, 105
Lobster Slaw with Teriyaki Shrimp, 67
Old Bay Shrimp Deviled Eggs, 87
Parmesan Crusted Tilapia, 63
Potato Chip Crusted Crab Cakes, 65
Saffron Mussels, 103
Shrimp Cocktail, 23
Spiced Clam Chowder, 145
Tempura Citrus Lobster Bites, 53
Wild Rice Stuffed Salmon, 92

Soups

Cauliflower Soup with Crispy Parsnips, 49
Cuban Black Bean Soup, 84
Roasted Tomato Bisque, 45
Spiced Clam Chowder, 145
Stadium Gumbo, 41
Thai Vegetable Soup with Tempura Vegetables, 144

Tomatoes

Fresh Tomato Marinara, 100

Vegetables

BBQ Black Beans, 134
Beer Batter Onion Rings, 120
Braised Asparagus with Roasted Garlic, 40
Garlic Mashed Cauliflower, 42
My Momma's Collard Greens, 91
Silver Queen Corn Ragout, 21
Smoke House Grilled Vegetables, 73
Spinach Fettuccine Alfredo, 104
Spinach with Crispy Garlic Chips, 123